The Complete Book of

Kitchen Collecting

Second Printing With Updated Price Guide

Barbara E. Mauzy

Schiffer Publishing Ltd

4880 Lower Valley Road, Atglen, PA 19310 USA

To Jimmy Mike because I love you!

Acknowledgments

Without the support of my family—Jim, Herb, and Elizabeth—this book could not have happened. For more than a year they allowed me to focus my time and energy on this project helping whenever and however they could.

There were other significant people who were a real part of this book. The following collectors and friends shared their treasures permitting me to photograph them for all to enjoy. Everyone of these wonderful people will have a special place in my heart always! THANKS to:

Elizabeth Mauzy
Lester Fawber/Thomas Dibeler
Lois Folino
David and Audrey Ann Krzeminski
Marge and Dennis Lerew
James G. Reigle
Brenda Sorber
Reta M. Stoltzfus
Patricia M. Zeman

Thanks go to Vivian and Jim Karsnitz for their help in book building. Their willingness to share made a real difference.

Also, thank you, Anita Dolphond from EKCO Housewares, Inc., for assisting in my research.

Every word of this book was typed and retyped, edited and reedited, printed and reprinted by my daughter, Elizabeth. She unselfishly gave up much of her summer vacation to work at the computer on my manuscript. Without her tireless efforts this book might not have been possible. A loving thank you to a wonderful daughter!

Library of Congress Cataloging-in-Publication Data

Mauzy, Barbara E.
The complete book of kitchen collecting / by Barbara E. Mauzy. -- 2nd printing with updated price guide.
p. cm.
ISBN 0-7643-2031-9 (pbk.)
1. Kitchen utensils--United States--Catalogs. I. Title.
NK6140.M38 2004
683'.82'075--dc22
2004004167

Revised price guide: 2004
Copyright © 1997 & 2004 by Barbara Mauzy

Designed by Bonnie M. Hensley
Cover design by Bruce Waters
Type set in Zurich XCn BT/Aldine 721 BT

ISBN: 0-7643-2031-9
Printed in China
1 2 3 4

Published by Schiffer Publishing Ltd.
4880 Lower Valley Road
Atglen, PA 19310
Phone: (610) 593-1777; Fax: (610) 593-2002
E-mail: Info@schifferbooks.com
Please visit our web site catalog at **www.schifferbooks.com**

In Europe, Schiffer books are distributed by Bushwood Books
6 Marksbury Avenue Kew Gardens
Surrey TW9 4JF England
Phone: 44 (0) 20-8392-8585; Fax: 44 (0) 20-8392-9876
E-mail: info@bushwoodbooks.co.uk
Free postage in the UK. Europe: air mail at cost.

This book may be purchased from the publisher.
Include $3.95 for shipping. Please try your bookstore first.
We are always looking for people to write books on new and related subjects.
If you have an idea for a book please contact us at the above address.
You may write for a free catalog.

Contents

Donated In Memory of

ALEXANDER STEWART

Introduction

The Beginning

A&J Manufacturing Company in Binghampton, New York, began its kitchen tool business in 1909 and became a nationally known manufacturer with chain stores across America. A&J was purchased by Ekco Housewares Company of Chicago in 1929 who, before this time, manufactured bread and cake pans and commercial items but not gadgets. This transition of ownership is evident on the variety of markings seen on pieces—"A&J," "EKCO A&J USA," "EKCO A&J," "EKCO USA."

The term "gadgets" only began being used in the 1920s when housewares became a thriving part of the economy. This word was borrowed from the French language and used by consumers and retailers alike.

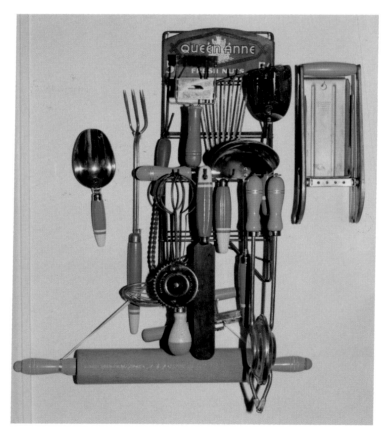

Age and Color

Customers often ask me, "Which is older, red or green?" The question of dating kitchenware is not a simple one to answer. After spending close to ten years buying and selling kitchen collectibles I took a serious look at locating accurate answers when working on this book. Hopefully the following information will provide some satisfaction for the curious collector.

Patent information is a source of dating objects but not always conclusively. The first patent number issued in 1920 was 1,326,899 and the last patent number issued in 1959 was 2,919,442. Therefore, pieces showing a patent number between these two numbers should be from the era presented in this book, right? And if 1,568,043 was a patent number issued in 1927 then that item was made in 1927, right? WRONG! A mechanism was patented in a particular year, but the handle treatment and color may have been altered annually. In other words, a piece marked with a patent number or date could have been made differently for several years making patent information an imperfect approach to determine the age of an item.

EKCO Housewares, Inc. in Illinois provided me with the history of their company and directed me to *The Housewares Story* by Earl Lifshey, published by the National Housewares Manufacturing Association and copyrighted in 1973. From this information I can perhaps answer some questions, but clear-cut definitive answers are not completely possible without digging through manufacturers' archives. (I did try to do that but to no avail.)

Before 1927 there was no consideration of using color in the kitchen. Three stores were involved in conceptualizing and marketing color—Macy's, John Wanamaker's, and Abraham & Straus. Primarily Macy's in New York City, and employee Joe Kasper, were responsible for color development and consumer acceptance with their "Color in the kitchen" program launched in 1927. Three colors began the revolution—Mandarin red, apple green, and Delft blue.

Manufacturers got involved in producing all kinds of kitchenware in colors, but the process was quite flawed. No color standards existed and even the paint was inconsistent. One company's red was a shade off from another company's red, and the same red was not reproduced accurately by a given company. Consumers were very unhappy. They clearly liked the idea of using color in their kitchens but demanded better quality control.

Professor Arthur Hardy invented the "colorimeter" to allow for consistent, accurate color reproduction and duplication around 1928. This was a help but handles were so varied that it became a practice across America for stores to actually repaint the handles of gadgets themselves before attempting to sell them thus insuring exact, consistent color in the pieces they offered for sale at their shop.

In the mid-1930s the Taylor System Incorporated proposed eighteen colors as the foundation for any other variations. This was seen as an attempt to simplify color possibilities. On September 16, 1937, the National Retail Dry Goods Association established six standard colors for kitchens—White, Ivory, Royal Blue, Kitchen Green, Delphinium Blue, and Red. Colors were finally standardized!

House & Garden magazine created new, "official" colors in 1946. They listed twenty-two acceptable colors that were to be considered and reconsidered annually. Some colors were added and others dropped as part of this yearly update that was based on consumer response and actual sales. Just as a footnote, in 1972 thirty-six colors were on this list.

So, which is older, red or green? They both began in 1927. Other dating information on the variations of colors and striping is perhaps waiting to be discovered in an archive somewhere.

From 1910 until World War II the development of plastics flourished, and the first issue of *Plastics* magazine was printed in March, 1926. By 1942 there were seventeen types of plastic although most of these were not suited for use on housewares and gadgets.

A Note From the Author

The focus of this book is on gadgets and items found in kitchens of the 1920s, 1930s, 1940s, and 1950s. All pieces showcased are non-electrical—only hand-driven mechanisms are presented. Pictured here is only a sample of the vast realm of collectible kitchenware. Only time and space limited the examples provided, mankind's ingenuity is limitless!

Remember, today's pleasures are tomorrow's treasures so happy hunting!

Stainless Steel

The earliest kitchen pieces were tin plated, then came nickel plating. Chrome plating and carbon steel were next. Carbon steel often discolored and rusted resulting in high maintenance by homemakers attempting to restore their kitchen tools' appearance. In 1921 Rogers Brothers issued the Ambassador pattern of flatware with stainless steel knife blades. If this was not the very first time stainless steel was utilized, then it was at least the first major marketing of stainless steel.

Bakelite

Dr. Leo Hendrick Baekeland discovered phenolic plastics while researching in 1909 and named his invention "bakelite." This material required high temperatures and heat in the mold fabrication. Because of this bakelite could not withstand heat and was not necessarily a good material on items that would be exposed to cooking temperatures.

Plastic

It wasn't long after the invention of bakelite until cold molded plastics were created. These were much more successful as handles on cooking gadgets because they tolerated higher temperatures than bakelite.

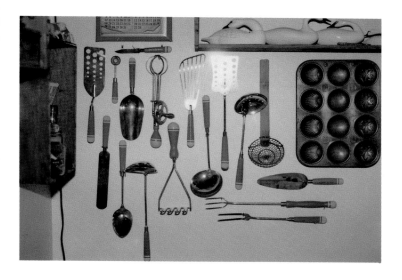

Beaters

Of primary concern when considering the value of a beater is its condition. Original paint and luster of all metal parts are highly regarded. Ease of use is essential.

The design and uniqueness of the item is also a major factor in its worth. Certain handle styles or mechanisms are less common and may be more collectible.

Value is also a dictate of popularity. Trends in decorating will enhance the worth of certain colored handles. Likewise, taste in materials used varies. Bakelite, wood, and older plastic are the most popular handle treatments. Collectors may make their selections by color, by handle material, by what they remember in a mother's or grandmother's kitchen, or simply by what they like.

Original packaging will enhance the value of a beater or other kitchen gadget. It may also provide a measure of charm to that item and probably guarantee a virtually unused condition.

Supply and demand has a significant impact on beaters and other kitchen implements. Undesirable color or material will have a negative impact on even a pristine handle.

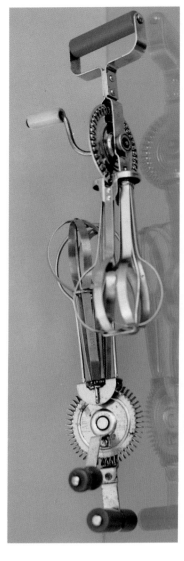

Here are two beaters with bakelite handles. Many people prefer the control provided in the design of the green beater. The beater on top is unique having bakelite handles in different colors. Green $40-45, red and yellow $55-60.

This Androck bakelite-handled beater is 12.5" long. The ribbed handle is designed to accompany bakelite "bullet" handles. A patent number of 2210810 dates this as 1940. $30-35.

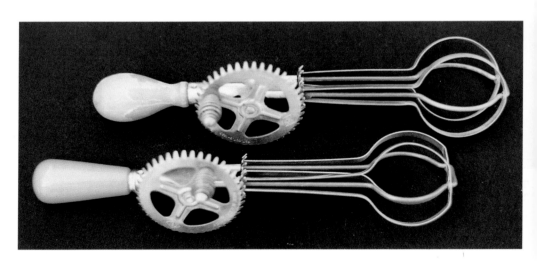

Both A&J beaters are patented Oct. 9, 1923, and are made in the U.S.A. Wear and missing paint will negatively effect the value of a wooden handled gadget. Good handle (front) $18-20, worn handle (back) $8-12.

A patent date of Oct. 9, 1923, is on this and many other A&J beaters. The design of this handle is one of the more popular ones often sought after by collectors of green kitchen items. $20-22.

The Edlund Company of Burlington, Vermont, manufactured this green beater. It is 11.5" in length. $18-20.

Ten inches long, this beater/whip is made in the U.S.A. and marked "Pat. Pending." Its unique design and pristine handle make it highly collectible. $35-40.

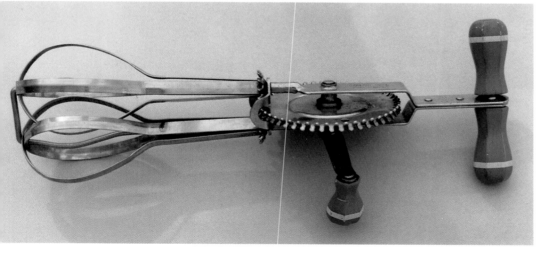

The "A&J Super Center Drive" beater is shown with an uncommon green handle treatment. This is marked "Stainless Steel" and "Bronze Bearings" and is made in the U.S.A. $28-30.

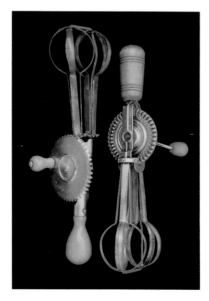

On the left is an A&J beater with the Oct. 9, 1923, patent date found on many of their beater mechanisms. The less common beater on the right is marked "Another Androck Product Made in United States of America." $12-15 each.

7

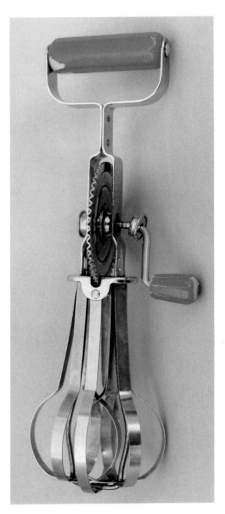

Damage to the original paint of this "High Speed Beater" will make it less desirable. It is 12.25" long and marked "A&J Made in United States of America Pat. Appld. for." $8-10.

"Made in U.S.A." is the only mark on this 12" long beater. $12-15.

Collectors of red handled items often prefer the handles having one (or more) white stripe(s) as shown. The beater pictured is "ECKO USA" and 10.75" in length. $12-15.

Red, gray, and white provide an uncommon treatment of the EKCO A&J "High Speed Super Center Drive Beater" handles. $12-15.

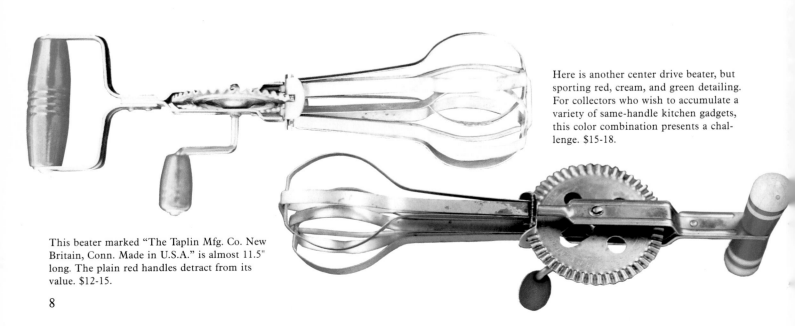

Here is another center drive beater, but sporting red, cream, and green detailing. For collectors who wish to accumulate a variety of same-handle kitchen gadgets, this color combination presents a challenge. $15-18.

This beater marked "The Taplin Mfg. Co. New Britain, Conn. Made in U.S.A." is almost 11.5" long. The plain red handles detract from its value. $12-15.

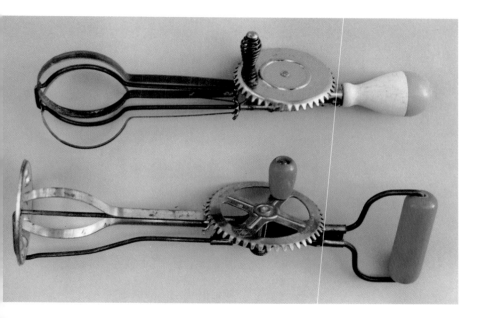

In red is an A&J beater/whip. This model marked "Pat. Oct. 9, 1923 Made in United States of America" is difficult to locate. The blue and white A&J beater has the same patent date. It is 10.75" long and is also a less commonly found item. However, the blue and white combination is not as popular with collectors as red and green. Red $35-40, blue $18-22.

The aqua, white, and black beater is 11.5" long. It is marked "High Speed Center Drive Beater EKCO A&J USA Pat. No. 2049727," a patent date from 1936. The general lack of interest in this color combination keeps its value low. $15-18.

These "High Speed Super Center Drive Beater(s) EKCO A&J" are identical in coloration but not in condition. The one on the right has more wear on both the wood and metal. Right $8-10, left, $12-15.

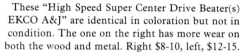

Barely any of the original yellow and green paint remains on this 12" long beater, thus lowering its value. It is marked "Another Androck Product Made in United States of America." $5-8.

Here are two more beaters patented Oct. 9, 1923. On the right is a pure white handle. White $10-12, red $12-15.

Arthur Beck Co., Chicago manufactured this "Whip Beater" in 1948. The one hand operation is a highly sought after design. Original packaging augment the value of this 11.5" tool. $40-45.

This 10.75" single hand beater was made in England. $30-35.

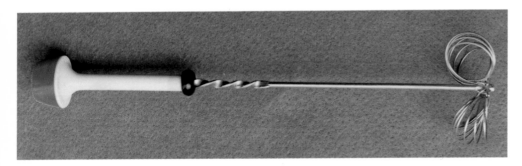

This "One Hand Wit Whip" has a black, white, and red handle in plastic. Other markings include "Made in U.S.A. Pats. 2096442, 2278394 and PND." The second patent date is from 1942. $20-25.

EKCO USA manufactured this 10.5" yellow handled beater. The same design was marketed in pink and turquoise. None command the price of the older, wire-type whip. $15-18.

The "Whippit" cream and egg whip is 13.5" long and pictured with a red and white swirl handle. Duro Metal Products Co. from Chicago also made this versatile beater in a green and white swirl and in plain brown. $15-20 plain brown, $40-45 red & white, $45-50 green & white.

Beaters were also manufactured for use with a variety of glass bases that often provided increments for liquid measurements. Some designs incorporated handles and/or pour spouts.

Condition and type of glass utilized will determine value. A two-piece unit with a beater top and decent clear base can still be purchased for $25.00. Transparent green glass, although more valuable than clear glass, is worth slightly less than jadite. Other more costly glass types include chailine (opaque Robin's egg blue), custard (opaque pearl white),

Seville (opaque pale yellow), and Delphite. Varieties, styles, and sizes are endless. This section provides several of the more common and affordable possibilities.

If you find yourself in a position of possessing either a top or bottom in search of a match it is recommended that you take along the piece owned while attempting to locate the needed item. A beater top may appear to fit a base by visual examination, but the key to correct fit is the ability of the mechanism to operate freely.

Both bases are embossed with measurement increments and have a capacity of two cups. The beaters are marked "A&J Made in the U.S.A." with Oct. 9-1923 patent dates. The green wooden handle is slightly more desirable. $70-75 each.

EKCO produced this clear two-cup measure with a beater top that stands 10.25" tall. $50-60.

Pictured is a transparent green two-cup measure with an A&J beater top patented Oct. 9-1923. $70-75.

The jadite and Delphite beaters stand almost 11.5" tall. They are marked "A&J Made In U.S.A. Pat. Oct. 9-1923." Jadite $90-100, Delphite $100-120.

The "Tip 'n Whip" beater and mixer provides an effortless mechanism in a secure, splash proof container. With an original label as pictured it is highly collectible, especially for display with red handled kitchen items. $65-70.

Hazel Atlas manufactured this beating jar with even numbered gradations of ounces from two through twelve. The unit is 9.25" tall when the beater is resting at the bottom of the jar. The glass is in exceptional condition considering that using the metal beater normally creates scratches inside. $35-45.

Taylor Churn Co. from St. Louis, Missouri, created the "Whixit." Ounces up to 24 are shown in pink. A pink plastic lid cradles a gray wooden knob. "Whixit" stands 9.25" high. $35-45.

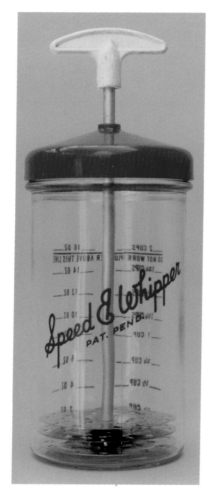

$2.50 would have purchased a "Speed - E - Whipper" from LB Sales Company in Los Angeles, California. The original paper insert exalts the versatility of the plastic lidded and handled beater, blender, and whipper. $25-35.

This SPEED-E-WHIPPER has been designed to save many minutes in the kitchen. It beats, blends, whips, ates, and homogenizes every time the plunger makes a complete cycle and you will enjoy using it to:

Whip Cream
Blend salad dressings
Mix malted milks
Beat eggs
Make smooth gravy
Make meringues
Mix cocktails
Blend smooth cake fillings
Mix delicious frostings
Children's formulas
Frozen Orange Juice

and many other uses you yourself will discover.

The SPEED-E-WHIPPER has been engineered to whip cream in a vacuum, forcing air into the cream which is the secret of the whipped cream staying durable for days without separating (over)

A red bakelite knob crowns the top of a "Jiffy Mixer." Hazel Atlas produced the glass for this 10" high unit patented in 1939. The sleek deco styling appeals to many collectors. $75-80.

Bowls

Whether for baking, cooking, serving, or storing, bowls are a kitchen essential. These functional items became an extension of the cook's personality—utilitarian, bold, massive, trendy.

Chosing bowls for one's collection is a matter of personal taste. Options include, but are not limited to, aluminum, plastic, pottery, Pyrex, jadite, and transparent glass. Consider whether or not the bowls will be used or only displayed. Most will not be microwave safe, and as is true with most older kitchen collectibles, they will require washing by hand.

A common feature of most bowls is the design allowing them to nest (or store) inside each other. In the space required to house the largest bowl of a set as many as six bowls will rest. Try using a doily or coffee filter between stacked bowls to retain optimum condition.

Fire King "Swirl" mixing bowls are probably the most popular of all jadite sets. Pictured is the complete five-piece nest that includes the rare 5" bowl worth $275 itself. The other bowls continue in size by one inch increments to the largest 9" bowl. Anchor Hocking made "Swirl" bowls in other colors, so those pieces are also included. Jadite $375-400, white $75-85, ivory $130-150 iridescent $50-60 (for the four largest bowls, set does not include 5" bowl).

This complete range set from the early 1950s is one of many produced by Anchor Hocking. It has three beaded rim bowls, salt and pepper shakers, and a grease jar. The metal tulip-design lids are marked "Anchor Hocking U.S.A." The bowls are marked "Fire King Ovenware" and measure 4.75", 6", and 7" across. The jadite set is difficult to assemble. This can be collected in white and ivory which is also pictured. $300-350 jadite, $175-200 white, $250-275 ivory.

This Anchorglass advertisement is undated—however, since Hocking Glass Company was begun in 1905 and the advertisement indicates "for 50 years" it may be from 1955. The nest of four "Swirl" bowls is shown with a 98 cent price.

Here are three of the four jadite "Splash Proof" bowls by Anchor Hocking. (Other Splash Proof sets follow.) Shown are the 7.5", 8.5", and 9.5" bowls. Missing is the elusive 6.5" bowl. 6.5", $100+; 7.5", $200; 8.5", $150; 9.5", $150.

Jeannette Glass Company made these 7" and 9" jadite bowls whose Delphite counterparts are pictured in this book. The bowls have vertical ribs partially up their sides and a star design radiating from the center of their bases. $75-80, 6"; $80-85, 7"; $80-85, 8"; $80-85, 9".

A distinctive bulge or "hump" on the sides of these bowls indicates McKee Glass as the manufacturer. These measure 6", 8", and 9" and were also made in white, custard, and fired-on colors. A yellow fired-on bowl is shown in this section. All cost less than the jadite. Jadite $45-50, 6"; $55-60, 7"; $65-70, 8"; $70-75, 9".

This is a complete "Red Dots" Splash Proof set from the mid-1950s. It includes four bowls measuring 6.5" to 9.5", a covered grease jar, salt and pepper shakers in two styles, and oil and vinegar cruets. The set has an ivory background, pure white is also available. Four bowls $200-250, grease $75-85, shakers $85-95, clear shakers $20-25, pair of cruets $35-40.

The counterpart to "Red Dots" is "Black Dots" shown as a complete set from the mid-1950s. Four bowls $200-250, grease $75-85, shakers $100-120.

Of all the Anchor Hocking Splash Proof sets, "Kitchen Aides" is among the most difficult to find. Shown are two views of the kitchen tools decorating all four bowls. Shakers and a grease jar are available but hard to locate. "Kitchen Aides" is from the late 1950s. Four bowls $350-400, grease $150-175, shakers $175-200.

"Ships" pieces are found throughout this book. Here are four mixing bowls with the distinctive "McK" marking on the base indicating McKee Glass Company. The bowls measure 6", 7", 8", and 9" and were made in the 1930s. Set of four, $150-175.

"Tulips" were made in white and ivory glass during the 1950s. Pictured are the grease jar and shakers with their distinctive tulip lids. The other shaker lids should have an "S" or "P" in script. The four matching bowls are shown in the next picture. Four bowls $200-250, grease $80-90, shakers $85-95.

Hazel Atlas produced this 6.5" bowl with stylized roosters. $15-18.

These four unmarked bowls were manufactured by Hazel Atlas. The diameters measure 8.25", 7", 5.75", and 4.75". Dinnerware including plates, mugs, tumblers, cups and saucers, and cereal bowls were made to accompany the nest of bowls. $60-75 for all four.

Both Seville (yellow) bowls are from McKee. The bowl on the left is identical to the custard bowl in the previous picture. The bowl on the right, which is also 9", is molded in the most commonly used McKee Glass Company design. $45-50 each.

McKee Glass Company produced these red dotted bowls. The measurements for this set are identical to "Ships" 6", 7", 8", and 9". These were made in the 1930s and 1940s. Set of four, $400-450.

McKee Glass Company made this 9" custard bowl. Custard, a rich off-white glass, is just gaining recognition among collectors. Look for custard prices to increase. $20-25.

This 9.5" unmarked bowl sports fired-on red polka dots. It is 5.75" deep. $40-45.

Collectors are sometimes surprised to learn that Pyrex made Delphite bowls. This one is 8.5" with a capacity of 2.5 quarts. $30-35.

Even if this bowl didn't have the signature "McK" on its base, the bulging shape indicates McKee Glass. The fired-on green stripes remain in exceptional condition. $75-85.

17

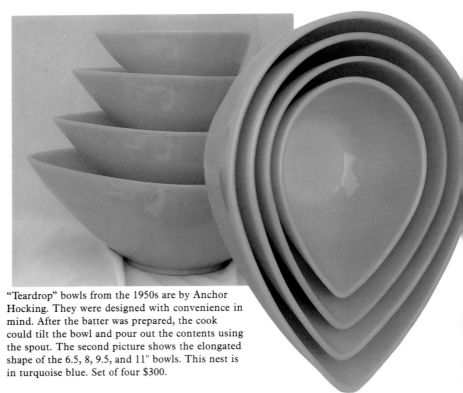

"Teardrop" bowls from the 1950s are by Anchor Hocking. They were designed with convenience in mind. After the batter was prepared, the cook could tilt the bowl and pour out the contents using the spout. The second picture shows the elongated shape of the 6.5, 8, 9.5, and 11" bowls. This nest is in turquoise blue. Set of four $300.

Three Jeannette Glass Company Delphite bowls match two jadite bowls previously pictured. Their diameters are 6, 7, and 8". 6", $110-120; 7", $75-85; 8", $80-90; 9" (not pictured), $90-100.

Jeanette Glass Company made these Delphite bowls that measure 9.5" and 7.5". 9.5", $90-100; 7.5" $75-85.

Measuring 7" and 9" these Delphite bowls are from McKee Glass. 7", $90-100; 9", $110-120.

"Teardrop" bowls were also made in jadite and white. The jadite bowls shown are 6.5 and 9.5", and the white "Teardrop" bowl is 6.5". These were introduced in 1956. Set of four jadite bowls $450, single white bowl $25-30.

Sapphire Fire King Utility bowls were made in three sizes—approximately 7, 8.25, and 10"—from 1942 through 1948. Anchor Hocking made dozens of items in this "OVEN-GLASS" including casseroles, measuring cups, and pie plates. Set of three $85.

Pictured are three of the five pink "Crisscross" bowls. Set of five $350.

Here is a complete set of "Crisscross" bowls in cobalt. Set of five $500.

"Crisscross" by Hazel Atlas Glass Company has bowls in five sizes and four colors: crystal (clear), transparent green, cobalt blue, and pink. Green is not pictured, but pricing is provided here. Crystal set of five $145, green set of five $400.

A nest of five cobalt bowls is by L.E. Smith. Of all the cobalt bowls pictured, this style is the most rare. Set of five $700-800.

The first picture shows a set of six cobalt blue Hazel Atlas bowls nested together, and the following picture separates them. The smallest and largest bowls can be a real challenge to find if piecing this nest together one bowl at a time. Set of 6 $350-400.

Hazel Atlas Glass Company made bowls in pink (and green) exactly like the cobalt bowls in the two previous pictures. The largest 11.75" bowl is not pictured. Set of six $200-250.

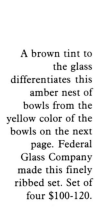

A brown tint to the glass differentiates this amber nest of bowls from the yellow color of the bowls on the next page. Federal Glass Company made this finely ribbed set. Set of four $100-120.

A finer vertical rib distinguishes the Federal Glass Company's mixing bowls from the Hazel Atlas bowls measuring from left to right 7, 9, 5, and 10.75". This is not a complete set. $30-35 each.

Two partial sets of Hazel Atlas Glass Company's "REST-WELL" bowls have broad, flat bases to "rest well" on counter tops. Complete nests have five bowls. Pink set of five $250-275, yellow set of five $300-350.

Hocking Glass Company produced a nest of six ribbed transparent bowls. The largest bowl measuring 11.5" is not pictured. Set of six $300-350.

The two pairs of bowls are from Hazel Atlas. On the right are "REST-WELL" bowls like those previously pictured in pink and yellow. Left set of six $200-250, right (REST-WELL) set of five $250-275.

McKee manufactured this yellow fired-on bowl. The yellow color was added to (actually fired onto) a white bowl. $30-35.

An advertisement from the June 1949 *Ladies' Home Journal* extols the virtues of a nest of Pyrex Mixing Bowls for $2.95. Today they are among the most recognized and collected bowls of all.

Pyrex continued production of their popular, durable bowls in a variety of solid colors and patterns. A nest of four pink bowls sold for $2.95 in 1956. Today it sells for $100-120. The stripes and polka dots are just now becoming popular again. Expect to pay $20-30 apiece for any of the bowls in these two pictures.

Yellow, green, red, and blue create the standard, original Pyrex set of mixing bowls. $85-100 set of four.

Collectors of Hull pottery may appreciate this 9.5" oven proof bowl. The fabulous colors —pink, black, and gray—provide an ideal piece for a "Fifties" look. $25-35.

Shawnee Pottery Company produced "King Corn" bowls from 1946-1954. They were three of many ceramic pieces with corn kernels and leaves. Variations in color exist as the company manufactured different lines of cornware. Set of three $120-130.

A 10" diameter makes these unmarked aluminum bowls ideal for serving. They are 4.5" deep. $15-25 each.

Colorful, fun, and very trendy, six unmarked aluminum bowls measure just over 5.75" in diameter. $20-30 for the set.

Bread Boxes

Hoosiers, Sellers, Oxfords, and other kitchen furniture often included a metal drawer for the purpose of storing bread. When these kitchen cabinets began to be considered old fashioned the birth of the decorative metal bread box occurred.

There are basically three designs of bread boxes. The first is a decorated box with a hinged lift-up top, usually of one solid color. The next design has a plastic or bakelite handle to lift up a lid that slides back inside the unit. The third style has stacked compartments with separate doors allowing access to the contents. These are the most difficult to find.

Most bread boxes were a part of matched sets that might include any or all of the following: canisters, match safes, trash cans, sifters, trays, and trivets. Selection of a bread box should involve consideration of color, condition, and coordinating accessories.

The original price of $1.19 is still stamped on the bottom of this 13.5 x 8.5 x 10.25" bread box. The matching canisters and cake server are pictured in this book. A wonderful graphic of clover utilizes red and green allowing it to coordinate with handles of either color. $30-40.

This unmarked bread box sports a stylized fruit motif. It was originally produced in red, as shown, and green. (The matching canisters are pictured in this book, and the sifters are photographed in both colors.) The lack of interest in the graphic negatively impacts its value. $15-20.

Slight wear in the green leaves will reduce the value of this geranium-decorated bread box. Look for the coordinating bread box and match safe in this book. $25-30 as shown, $30-40 if mint.

Decoware manufactured this 13.75 x 9.75 x 8.25" apple bread box in one of the most popular graphics of all. Variations include white, buff, and yellow backgrounds. Look for coordinating accessories throughout this book. $40-45.

Collectors of red, green, and yellow can decorate with the versatile rose and checkered design of the unmarked bread box shown. The 14 x 9.25 x 6.5" unit was a bargain at its original price of 98 cents. $25-30.

Nesco embossed its name directly on the white plastic handle of the slide open door. Measuring 15 x 12 x 7.5" a green bread box is harder to locate than red. $20-30.

The 1951 copyright is printed on Necso Inc.'s hard-to-find Dutch design bread box (and matching canisters). A broad spectrum of colors provides a storage item compatible with many color schemes. $45-50.

In virtually 12 x 12 x 12" one is provided two sections of storage in an unmarked bread box with vented sides. A cake saver and canister set were made to match. Although fruits and vegetables are popular decorating themes, this unit lacks the bold colors many collectors often prefer. $35-45.

No manufacturer is shown on this 15.5 x 10 x 6.75" slide open bread box. Its simplicity of all red with a white handle popularizes it with collectors of red and white. $30-40.

This is the same geranium design shown previously on a lift-top bread box. The top door opens upward, and the bottom door comes down when unlatched. Wear reduces the value. $35-45 as shown, $65-75 if mint.

Butter Dishes

Butter dishes are found in three sizes: one pound, long quarter pound, and chunky quarter pound. The one pound butter dish will store a solid, rectangular block of butter. A quarter pound unit is designed for a stick of butter.

Selecting a butter dish for display or use might be based on the material of which it is made or the availability of companion pieces. Materials utilized in butter dishes range from glass to plastic. Many are made as part of a set of kitchen items. "Crisscross" includes bowls (as shown in a previous section), pitchers, tumblers, and more. The ivy design has

matching refrigerator dishes. "Ships" collectors will find shakers, bowls, canisters, and other treasures. (Look throughout the book for "Ships!")

Condition will affect the value of a butter dish as well as its availability in the marketplace. Remember that grandma never expected us to value and collect her butter dish, so be forgiving when considering condition. A small nick is use, not abuse. Perfection is next to impossible to find so be prepared!

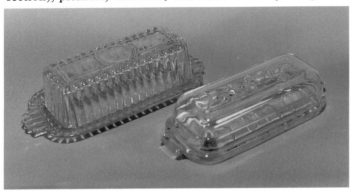

Both clear glass quarter pound butter dishes have matching clear glass refrigerator dishes. $12-15.

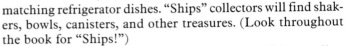

"Crisscross" by Hazel Atlas has butter dishes in a one pound and quarter pound size. Butter dishes come in four colors. The prices for quarter pounders are provided here. Crystal $30, green $60, cobalt $150, pink $90.

One pound butter dishes and 3.5 x 5.75" refrigerator dishes can be confusing to new "Crisscross" collectors. (Look in the "Refrigerator Dishes" section for more information.) The butter dish has tabs on the base that extend .25" from the rim. Crystal is the only color commonly seen. Crystal $25, green $50, cobalt $160, pink $90.

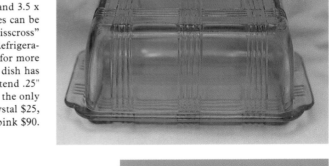

"Ships" by McKee was produced in red and black, but black is hard to find. This popular pattern has many options for the collector. Select pieces with a dark red (or black) color still showing a sheen. Red $75, black $175.

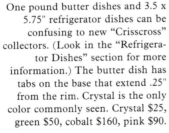

Nineteen cents purchased a "Genuine Burrite Ware" butter dish for quarter pound chunky sticks in the 1950s. This plastic butter dish was advertised to "keep butter clean (and) daisy-fresh." Burrite Ware is a trademark of Burroughs Mfg. Corp., Los Angles. $12-14 in unused condition.

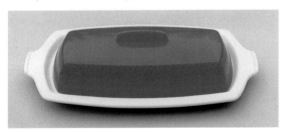

Steeds produce this 8" long, 2" high plastic quarter pound butter dish. (Look for more Steeds in the Plastic section of this book.) $12-14.

Cake Savers

Does anyone still bake layer cakes? For those of you with time and talent, here are cake savers to protect your creations. For the rest of us, most cake savers are companion pieces to canisters, bread boxes, match safes, and other kitchen accessories. Of the various storage items cake savers seem to have survived with the least abusive damage. Maybe grandma didn't bake that often, either!

The "Lady in the Garden" motif is a very popular design found on many metal accessories. (Look for the matching trash can in this book.) The cake saver has a 13.5" diameter and stands 5" tall. Although attractive, the protruding red knob on the lid limits decorating possibilities. $35-40.

This graphic should look familiar to you! The unmarked cake saver has a diameter of 12.5" and height of 6". $35-40.

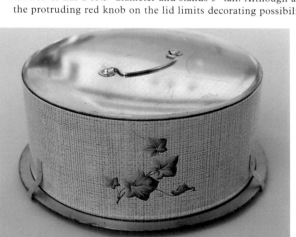

Ivy is once again a popular decorating theme. Decoware created this 11.75" diameter cake saver with lock down tabs enabling the user to carry his/her goodies by the handle. It stands 5.25" tall. $30-35.

Still popular today as a decorating accent, fruit adorns this unmarked cake saver. It is 11.5" across and 6" tall. $25-30.

Decoware created this pine cone motif cake saver. A matching bread box and canister was also produced. This measures 11.75" in diameter and 6" in height. $30-35.

A Pennsylvania Dutch design decorates the lid of a cake saver found in Maine. What makes this unique is the smaller size of only 9" across and 4" high. It was also made in a larger, more standard size. $20-25 either size.

Bright flowers create a glorious burst of color on this unmarked cake saver. It has a diameter of just under 11" and a height of 6.5". $35-40.

This three section unit stands 10" tall allowing a layer cake and two pies to stack neatly, occupying minimal kitchen space. It is 11.25" across and unmarked. Note the glass knob on the lid. The colors and knob place this as a late 1920s or early 1930s piece. $35-40.

An enamel cake saver is uncommon, and this one is in wonderful condition. Red and white purists will appreciate its simplicity. The diameter is 13.25" and the height is 6". $40-45.

The enamel cake saver previously pictured is part of this display which includes a bread box presented earlier in this book.

There can be no doubt as to the use of this copper-colored aluminum item. West Bend designed the lid to lock into the base for freshness and mobility. It is 14.5" across and 7" tall. $30-35.

Lustro-ware produced this "LOCKING CAKE COVER SET STOCK No. L-82 PAT. PEND. MADE IN U.S.A. COLS. PLASTIC PROD. INC. COLS. O." The bright red plastic and strong deco lines make this a very collectible cake saver. $40-45.

The base of this unmarked plastic cake saver is 13" square. Its right handle hinges down to unlock or lock the lid. When locked, the saver and contents can be transported securely using the gray plastic handle on the lid. $40-45.

Canisters

The practicality of older kitchen collectibles is evident in canister sets. Most were designed with four matching containers that nest inside one another when not in use. Precious kitchen storage or work space is not wasted on unused canisters.

From the largest to the smallest, canisters are normally thought to hold flour, sugar, coffee, and tea. Sets have fairly standard height dimensions of approximately 7.5", 6.5", 5.75", and 5.25".

Decoware is the most common manufacturer, and any of these canister sets do have a variety of matching accessories. This makes collecting an array of coordinating pieces a possibility if not a reality.

When selecting a canister set consider condition first. Remove the lid of each piece and look for rust. Examine the outside of each container noting wear, discoloration, and dents. Then, factor in the availability of companion pieces if you wish to assemble a variety of matched items.

In the late 1920s and early 1930s canister sets were often designated as "Flour" and "Sugar" containers. They were color coordinated to match the wooden kitchen cabinets that served as the baking center of the kitchen. Ever functional and practical, they were plain and undecorated. FLOUR is 7.25" tall, and SUGAR is 6" tall. Both are unmarked. $35-40 each.

Decoware created the ever-popular apple canister set. The background can be white as shown, yellow, or buff as in the next example. $40-45.

Two more Decoware canister sets are the apples with a buff background and poppies. The poppies have large blossoms in the front and one smaller flower on either side. The back of each of the four poppy canisters is blank. Apples $45-50, poppies $35-40.

The ivy-decorated tin shown served as a storage canister, and the lid became a serving tray. Its dual function exemplifies practicality of design. The canister measures 12.25" tall and 11" across and is an unmarked single unit not part of a set. $25-35.

The popular 1950s colors of pink and black are evident in the Decoware set. Three additional canisters are nested inside. $35-40.

Flowers and a checkered base combine to create a brightly colored unmarked canister set. $45-50.

A display of antherium are on these Decoware canisters. Notice the knob on each lid as an addition to more recent sets. Chances are pretty good that the person opening these canisters would still have to use fingernails around the edges of the lids. $35-40.

Canister sets in yellow are less common but not highly sought by today's collectors. Decoware also produced this set. $40-45.

Ransburg from Indianapolis created a canister set with metal bases and plastic lids. This lid design is much simpler to use than the knobs found on Decoware items. $40-45.

Fruit as a decorating motif is presented on this Decoware set. The bold, bright graphic makes this a colorful addition to a collector's kitchen. $35-40.

NC Colorware made these wonderful clover canisters. The vivid colors and plaid trim blend effectively with red or green, as shown in the following photograph. $40-45.

A copyright date of 1951 appears on these Nesco. Inc. canisters. Dutch designs continue in popularity today. $60-65.

A bouquet decorates each canister in this unmarked set. $40-45.

This colorful canister set is by NC Colorware. The labels are not original from the manufacturer but decals added by a past owner. $40-45.

A floral and plaid design creates a subdued look on these unmarked canisters. Pink and purple blossoms provide an unusual pallet. $35-40.

Here are three of the four pieces of an unmarked set. Although it is incomplete and in substandard condition the design is uncommon and worth noting. Each container has its own farm scene done in bright yellow, red, and green. A complete, well-preserved set would be a delightful find! $60-65 if mint and complete.

The lids of these three canisters have red bakelite knobs and are hinged on the back. The FLOUR and SUGAR measure 8.5" high and 5.25" deep and wide. Both have "52"on the bottom. The TEA canister is 7.25" tall and 4.25" deep and wide with "51" on the bottom. Kreamer patented these unusual pieces. $15-20 each.

Parker Metal Dec. Co. from Baltimore, Maryland, manufactured this single canister. It has unusually small dimensions being 5.5" tall and 3.5" across. Markings include "PARMECO." $10-15.

Choppers

There is an endless variety of choppers that have been manufactured. My experience with collectors is that they base a purchase selection on handle color and/or design or on past personal knowledge of the chopper. "That's the kind my mother (or grandmother) used!" is something I often hear exclaimed at a moment of discovery. People who actually use their old kitchen gadgets usually prefer them to new ones.

Chopper handles can be wood, metal, or bakelite in any number of colors. The blades can be single, double, or triple.

Foley created a "spring" chopper with three blades. There are any number of "chopper jars" from which to select. Knobs for these will be found in wood, plastic, or bakelite.

I've included mincers in this section since mincing and chopping are similar cooking tasks.

The choppers presented provide a sampling of handles and blades. If selecting one to use, look for stainless steel blades in good condition.

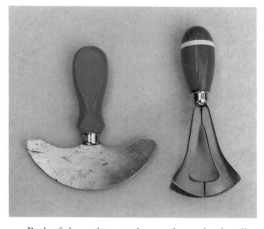

Both of these choppers have red, wooden handles. The flat handled, unmarked item on the left is 5" high and 4.5" across. EKCO A&J U.S.A. manufactured the 6" long chopper on the right. $10-14 each.

These choppers have bakelite handles. The common red unit is manufactured by Corona and is almost 6" long. Corona produced a large variety of good quality bakelite handled kitchen utensils. The uncommon black chopper is manufactured by Androck and is almost 4" across the handle and 3.5" high. The finely ribbed texture of the black handle is indicative of the "bullet" handle design of some bakelite gadgets. Both choppers have stainless steel blades. Red $18-20, black $25-30.

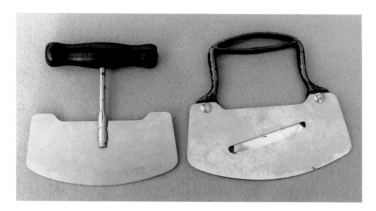

Of the colors being collected today, black is the least popular. If anyone knows why, please share the reason. Black works wonderfully in modern all-white kitchens and belongs with pink and gray or red and white. The wooden handled chopper on the left is 5" from top to bottom, the handle being 3.75" long. The metal handled chopper on the right is marked "Japan." It is 5.25" from top to bottom and 5.5" across. Both choppers have blades marked "Stainless Steel." $8-12 each.

Although unmarked, this chopper seems to be a variation of the red EKCO A&J chopper in the first and following pictures. Note the original price of 25 cents stamped on the handle. $12-14.

Six inches in length, here is another EKCO U.S.A. chopper. $8-12.

This chopper is marked "Stainless Steel" on the blade and is 5.5" long. The condition of the painted handle is only fair, but this chopper is an unusual one. $18-22 if mint, $8-12 as shown.

Here are two wooden handled, double bladed choppers. The red one is marked "ACME MGM Co. Stainless Steel" and is 5.25" tall. The green chopper is marked "A&J Made in U.S.A." and is 4.25" tall. This one is very seldom found. Red $10-15, green $30-35.

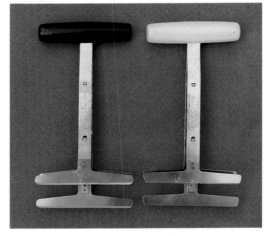

The Foley Chopper is the most popular of all the choppers I sell. Here are five handle colors and two handle styles. They are 7.75" long. $12-14 each regardless of color.

The "Tearless Onion and Vegetable Chopper" comes from Newark, New Jersey, and has a red wooden handle. $25.

Chopper jars are like early food processors. The contents being reduced remain neatly inside the glass. Amounts are readily determined with embossed units of measurements. A small wooden disk should be in the base of the jar to act as a shock absorber when in use. From left to right the handles are: red plastic, red wood, red bakelite, orange bakelite, and yellow wood. All have a 1.5 cup capacity. Red plastic $10, red wood $15, red bakelite $25, orange bakelite $40, yellow wood $15.

This partial label remains on the base of a chopper jar.

An "Aurora Food Chopper" label is still easy to read. Original labels add to the value of kitchen items but make them difficult to use. $25.

A chopper jar in transparent green glass is a rare find. This stands 12" tall and is marked "Lorraine Metal Mfg. Co. Inc. New York City, N.Y." on the base of the glass. $65

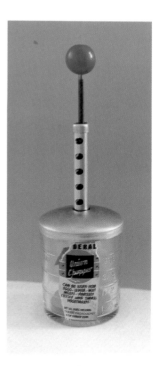

This "Federal Onion Chopper" is 10.75" tall with a red wooden handle. $25.

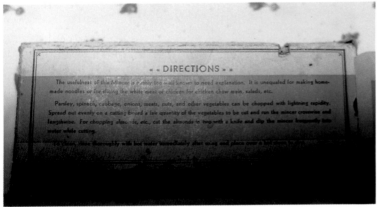

This unmarked mincer is just over 7.5" long. The poor condition of the metal decreases its value. $5-7 as shown. $8-10 if mint.

Here are the front and back of "THE ACME MINCER" box with a mincer. $15-18 with box, $10-12 without box.

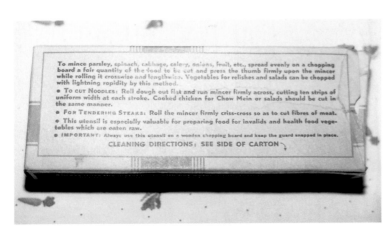

"THE ACME ROTARY MINCER" box is dated 1935. The tool is the same as "The Acme Mincer," but the packaging is different. $15-18 with box, $10-12 without box.

Cleaning Tools

After cooking or baking comes cleaning. Here are a few varied items from the past designed to ease the burden.

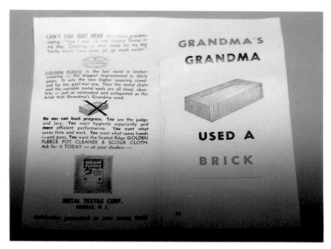

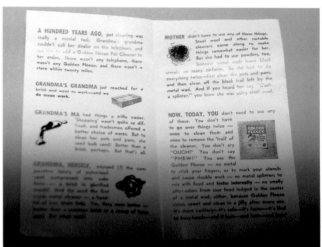

"The Improved Sealed Edge Golden Fleece" sold for 10 cents per 5 x 5.5" cloth. This unused box of three dozen is prized as unused store stock. $25-35 box and contents.

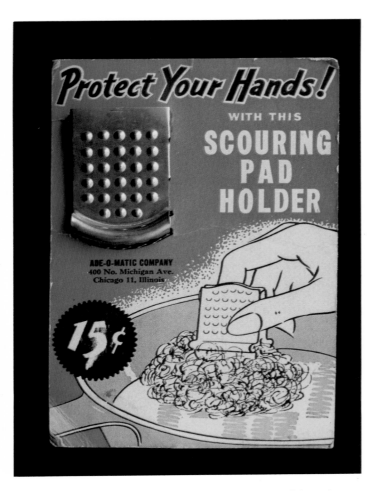

Cherries and cherry blossoms decorate a metal dust pan in unusually good condition. $15-20.

Fifteen cents would purchase this "Scouring Pad Holder" from the Ade-O-Matic Company of Chicago. The tool measures 2.25 x 1.5". $18-20 with package, $5-7 without package.

A wonderful green handle remains on this unique wire bristled brush. It is 8.25" long. $20-25.

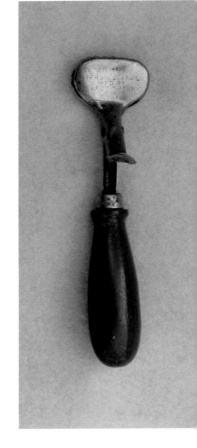

This tool marked "SURHOLD UTENSIL CLEANER Mfd. By select Spts. Co. N.Y.C. U.S.A." is 5.5" in length. $12-15.

Cookie Cutters

The assortment of cookie cutters seems almost infinite. Materials used and shapes created are as varied as cookie recipes. Cutters may be metal or plastic. Handles may be wood, metal, or plastic. Shapes include many geometric forms as well as figurals in recognizable and unknown characters.

Clubs, spades, hearts, and diamonds (the four suits) were often sold in sets for sandwich cutting. This was meant to add a touch of ambiance to a card party.

The most recent favorite of many collectors are the plastic cutters that advertise a product. A price of $1.00 three years ago may now be $10.00 for a single item. Look for U.S.A. on older plastic cookie cutters. The newer ones are marked Hong Kong.

Different green wooden handles are on three circular cookie cutters. On the far left is the "bullet" or "acorn" handle. $4-5 each.

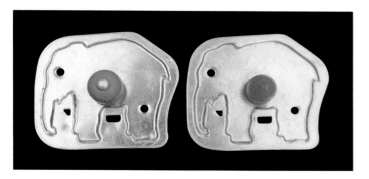

These elephants are among the hardest to find wooden handled metal cookie cutters. They are 3.5" across from trunk to tail and shown with two different handle treatments. $15-20.

Diamond shaped cookies cutters were often part of sandwich cutter sets. Here are five variations with green wooden handles. $4-5 each.

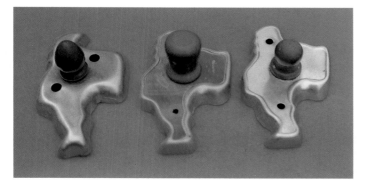

The three Santa Claus cookie cutters have different green handles. Santa in the center has the worn remains of his original paper. Left and right $10-12, center (with paper) $12-18.

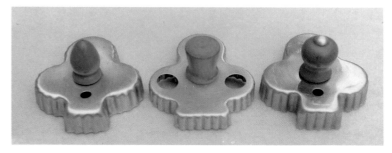

These club cookie cutters were often included in sandwich cutter sets. $4-5 each.

A green "bullet" handle is on a flower having a 2.5" diameter. $4-5.

Four flags have "bullet" handles but the metal on the shiny flags is aluminum and on the darker ones is tin. $20 each.

All four stars have different handles. $4-5 each.

Sandwich cutter sets often included heart cookie cutters. $6-8 each.

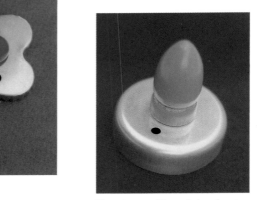

Here is a cookie and doughnut cutter with a massive green handle. $5-7.

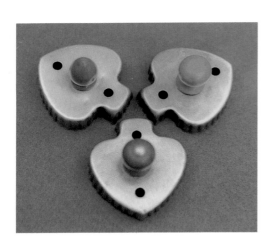

Spade cookie cutters were often included in sandwich cutter sets. $4-5 each.

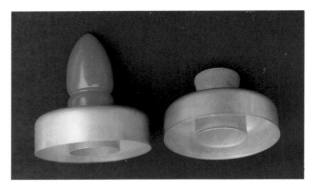

This view shows the removable center circles in two cookie and doughnut cutters. These centers rotate slightly and pull away from two screws. The popular large "bullet" on the left is in excellent condition while the handle on the right shows much wear. Left $5-7, right $2-3 as shown, $4-5 if mint.

Both axes have "bullet" handles. $8-10 each.

Three red "bullet" handles are on three different shapes. The club and spade cookie cutters may have been part of sandwich cutter sets. $4-5 each.

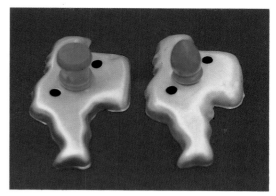

These two Santa Claus cutters are identical except for their handles. $10-12 each.

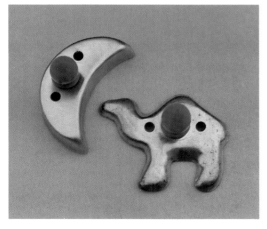

The very collectible Scotty is shown with two different red wooden handles. $10-12 each.

This all-metal lion is 4.5" long. $5-7.

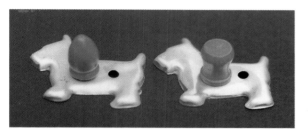

Red "bullet" handles are on two different circular cookie cutters. $4-5 each.

The bend in the handle of the star is original, not damage from use. Figurals such as the chicken are more valuable than geometric shapes. Chicken $5-7, circle and star $5-7 each.

One of the most sought after cookie cutters is the camel with a "bullet" handle. It is 3.25" from nose to tail. The crescent moon is also very popular and difficult to find. Camel $15-20, moon $8-10

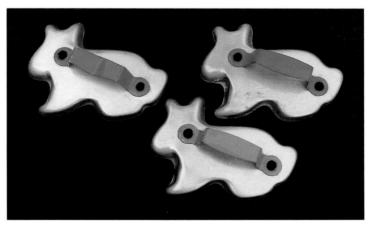

Three 4" long rabbits have different handles. $5-7 each.

The "In-Genia Rotating Cutter" is from West Germany. A side panel of the box boasts "5 different appetizing shapes with 1 rotation. Just whisk roller across Dough or Bread." $15-20 without box, $20-25 as packaged.

Wear-ever produced the "Lazy Susan Cooky Cutter" which sold for $1.50. Five shapes are provided on this handy tool. $15-20 without box, $20-25 as packaged.

A six-sided box holds fourteen plastic cookie cutters. This set was made by Hutzler Mfg. Co. in Long Island City, New York. $25-30 packaged set, $1-1.50 each if purchased individually.

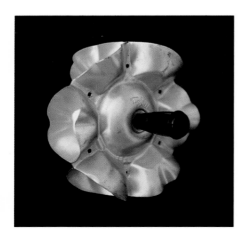

Six shapes are on a Foley cookie cutter with black plastic handles. It measures 4.5" across. $15-20.

The complete Hansel and Gretel Cookie Cutter Set is still in an original box. $30-35 as packaged, $4-5 each if purchased individually.

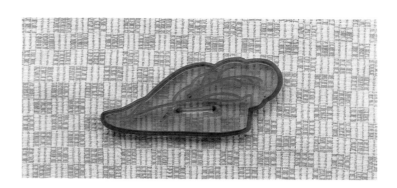

American-made plastic cookie cutters are gaining in popularity. The cartoon cat is marked "Copyright Loew's Incorporated, 1956." Santa is by "Life-Like," and the tree is from "HRM." Cat $7-10, Santa $4-6, tree $2-3.

Robin Hood's hat is from Robin Hood's Flour. Various plastic cookie cutters in assorted colors were produced as advertising premiums for Robin Hood's Flour and other companies. $12-15.

A 3.75" tall plastic cutter is marked "Betty Crocker Gingerbread Mix Made in U.S.A." $5-7.

Both of these figural plastic cookie cutters have double handles and are marked "PAT. PEND." $7-10 each.

This is the American-made "KO Biscuit and Cookie Cutter." It is 2" across and 2.75" tall. When the handle on top is depressed the batter or dough is pushed from the cutter. $15-20.

The 4" long rabbit's head is marked "HRM MADE IN U.S.A." It has a single handle. The unmarked double-handled elephant is 4.5" from trunk to tail. $7-10 each.

Rochow Swirl Mixer Co., Rochester, New York, created a six-piece "Doughnut and Cookie Cutter Party Set." The 1", 1.25", 1.5", 1.75", 2", and 2.25" "Fingergrip" cutters nest inside of each other. $15-20 as packaged, $10-15 set of six without package.

Here is a fabulously creative use of cookie cutters: the cupboard handles in this kitchen are all cookie cutters. The main pantry and top cabinets have "bullet" handles painted blue. The bottom doors which are in the work space have aluminum cutters with less obtrusive handles. Each cutter is screwed into the cabinetry using the holes machined into it.

Coring Tools

Coring tools measure from 4.5" to 6.5" and come in a variety of styles and handle treatments. They are not hard to find so select one with all parts and materials in good condition.

Some gadgets were cleverly designed to do more than one job. For this reason, look for other corers with the garnishing tools.

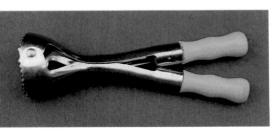

Yellow handles are on a 5.25" long coring tool that is unmarked. $7-10.

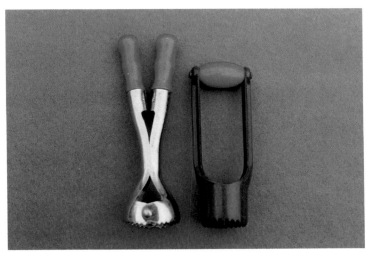

Both of these coring tools are metal with red wooden handles. They are unmarked. $7-10 each.

Here are two more coring tools with red wooden handles. The one on the left is marked "Citra Products Winter Haven, FLA. Stainless Steel Pat. 050794." The corer on the right is mostly plastic. No manufacturer is indicated but "Pat. Pend. Made in U.S.A." is inscribed. Left (metal and wood) $7-10, right (plastic and wood) $5-7.

Nutbrown's signature silver stripes decorate this light blue "Butter Pat Marker and Apple Corer." It was made in England. $15-20.

A price of fifty cents is printed on the end panel of this box. It is advertised as "all metal" but the handle is red wood. $12-18 with box, $7-10 without box.

Kovac's Products, Inc. N.Y. made this coring tool with an unusual forest green wooden handle. It is 4.75" long. $7-10.

Corn Poppers

Non-electric corn poppers are fairly standard item to item. Nominal differences occur in the overall length, the dimensions of the basket, and the color of the handle.

Selection should be based on handle color and overall condition. The screen-like mesh of the basket tends to rust, so be sure to examine this area carefully.

This green handled corn popper is 25" long. $20-25.

This blue handled corn popper is 24" long. $20-25.

This red handled corn popper is 26" long. $20-25.

Dough Blenders

Few kitchen gadgets can be considered as simple yet helpful as a dough blender. It does just as its name indicates, with five rows of serrated surfaces to work into the ingredients being combined.

Included in this section are wire blenders. These have a similar design as dough blenders but lose effectiveness with thick batter.

Handles may be bakelite or wood in a variety of colors, otherwise, these are fairly standard items. Look for original paint in good condition if purchasing a wooden handle. All brands measure about 4" across the handle.

"Androck Made in U.S.A." is on the red handled wire blender. Plain red wood is a common handle treatment. $6-8.

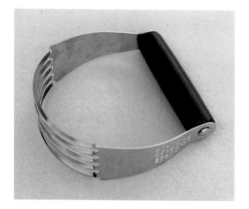

This black handled tool is marked "Chromium Plated EKCO U.S.A. Dough Blender to blend flour with shortening." $7-10.

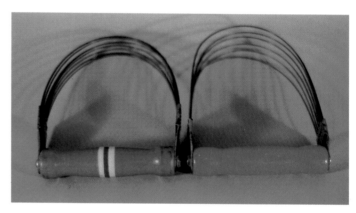

A patent date of 11-12-29 appears on two Androck blenders. The wooden handles are 4" long. Left (green) $12-15, right (plain red) $7-10.

"A&J Made in the U.S.A." is on this yellow and green dough blender. The handle condition is not pristine, but the color combination is less common. $7-10.

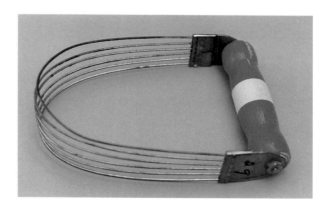

The original 29 cent price is crayoned on the side of this Androck blender. $12-15.

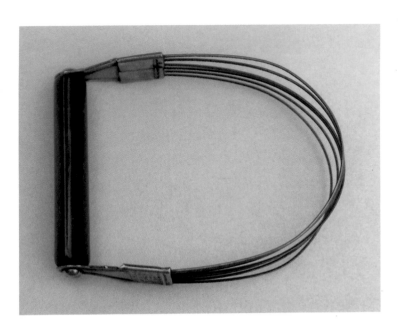
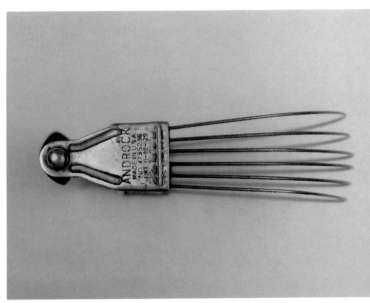

Androck patented this blender with a bakelite handle on 11-12-29. $25-30.

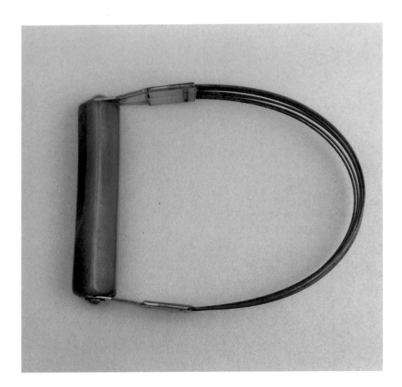
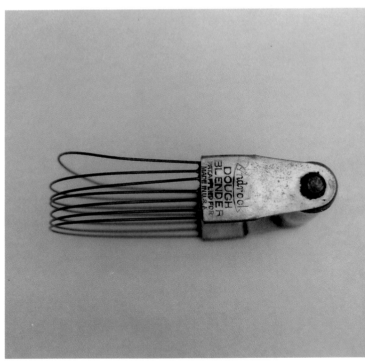

A bakelite handle is on Androck's Dough Blender. $25-30.

Egg Cups

An entire book has already been written devoted to egg cups. Presented here is just a sample of the broad scope of possibilities from plain to figural. The materials used for these colorful, fun items include ceramics, transparent glass, opaque glass, pottery, milk glass, wood, chalk, plastic, and celluloid.

Lines, cracks, chips, and wear will negatively effect the value of an egg cup. Be sure to examine all edges and surfaces carefully before making a purchase.

Wooden egg cups are hard to find in good condition as the paint has a tendency to chip off the surface. The girl's head is unmarked. The bunny is marked "Made in German Democratic Republic VEB HOLZWAREN GAHLENZ." $15-20 each.

All five egg cups shown are unmarked Stangl pieces. Many more Stangl egg cups are available to accompany dinnerware patterns. They are almost 3.5" tall and 2.5" across the opening. $10-15 each.

Here are five solid-colored egg cups in a variety of materials. They are priced left to right: Chailine $10-15, jadite $20-25, light green ceramic $8-12, gold ceramic $8-12, white china $3-5.

The hen and rooster egg cups are made of milk glass. They are about 3.5" tall. The hen is 3.25" across her opening, and the rooster is just over 2.5" across his opening. $15-20 each.

Transparent green glass egg cups are unusual, and collectors of green Depression Glass may find these particularly desirable. They are 4.25" tall with a block-type design. $18-20 each.

The hat on the clown is removable but acts as a lid to maintain the temperature of its contents. The egg cup with lid measures 4" tall. The accompanying salt and pepper are 2" tall. Set $45-50.

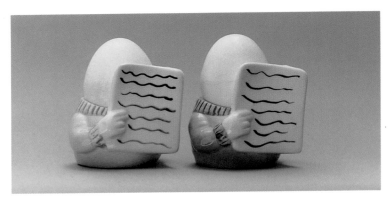

The two "people" egg cups are unmarked. $10-15 each.

The figural elephant is unmarked. The duck is stamped "JAPAN" on its base. They are about 2.5" tall. $15-20 each.

A "JAPAN" sticker is located on the bottom of each of these egg cups. Flowers decorate the outsides and pastel hues line the insides. $5-10 each.

The plastic Humpty Dumpty is marked "REG 875216 876006" and is 2.75" tall. The celluloid rooster is marked "Made in England" and is just over 2" tall. These materials are less common than pottery, glass, and ceramics. $20-25 each.

Roosters and chickens continue to be popular kitchen "critters." The three egg cups shown are all from Japan and only 2.25" tall. $10-15 each.

Three nursery rhymes are depicted on these unmarked egg cups. "Mary Quite Contrary," "Little Miss Muffet," and "Little Boy Blue" stand just over 2" in height. $10-15 each.

Both the pig with a fiddle and the roses appear to be from the same mold. They are 2.25" tall, 1.75" across the opening, and stamped "JAPAN." pig $8-12, roses $5-10.

The chalk chicken is 3" tall and the colorful rooster is 3.5". Both are unmarked, and the rooster appears to have hatched in a ceramics studio. Chicken $20-25, rooster $5-10.

Here are four egg cups each about 2.5" tall. The barn and the flowers are marked "JAPAN," and the other two egg cups are unmarked. Barn $8-12, rooster $8-12, flowers $5-10, monogram $3-5.

"Japan" stickers remain on the couple in the center while "Fanny Farmer" is embossed on the egg cups at either end. Chicks $10-15, people $10-15 each, rooster $15-20.

The unmarked figural rooster measures 4" tall at his head. $15-20.

At just over 3.5" these egg cups are taller than many. The dancing couple have a sponge-ware background and no markings. The rooster is marked "JAPAN." $10-15 each.

The redware cat on the left is 3" tall. The egg cup on the right looks like an "egghead." However, close examination shows missing paint where there is white. The head was probably a vegetable design. $15-20 cat, $8-12 person as shown, $15-20 if mint.

The unmarked chef is 3.75" tall. $10-15.

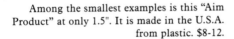

Among the smallest examples is this "Aim Product" at only 1.5". It is made in the U.S.A. from plastic. $8-12.

A salt shaker head rests inside this colorful unmarked egg cup measuring 5.5". It probably has a "pepper head" mate in a similar design. $20-25.

An advertisement in the April 1948 *Ladies' Home Journal* for Simtex cloths includes two "Aim Product" egg cups.

52

Forks

Forks provide a variety of functions, and so were produced in an assortment of configurations. They will be found in many lengths and colors with differing prong sizes, shapes, and amounts.

Plastic, wood, and bakelite were the most common handle materials, and their condition should be of primary focus when making a purchase. Chromium and stainless steel were usually the metals used for the shaft and prongs. Select forks whose metals have retained good shine and have resisted rust or other deterioration.

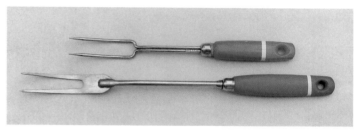

EKCO U.S.A. made the 9.25" long fork on the top. The 13" long fork on the bottom is from A&J. $10-15 each.

Blue and white handles in good condition are hard to find. This fork is 15.5" long and in virtually unused condition. The red handled fork is pictured at its 19" length but will extend to 29.5". $10-15 each.

The three-pronged fork is .25" longer than the two 13" forks. It is marked "A&J Made in United States of America." The two-pronged forks are marked "A&J EKCO USA." Three prongs $10-12, two prongs $7-10 each.

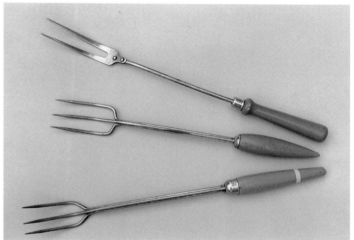

The darkest green handled, two-pronged fork on top is the only one marked. It is 13.75" long and manufactured in the U.S.A. by DURO. The "bullet" handled, 12.25" fork in the middle tends to be a less popular handle treatment overall. The bottom fork is 13.5" long. $10-15 each.

This 12" long red handled fork is unmarked. $10-15.

Here are two colors, four handle designs, and four prong arrangements. The varieties are endless! The top red handled fork is 12.5" long and marked "A&J Made in the United States of America." It hosts an unusually long handle. The other red handled fork is by Androck and is almost 10" long. The 12.75" black handled fork is unmarked. HYCO manufactured the smaller 8.25" black handled fork. A&J red $10-15, others $7-10 each.

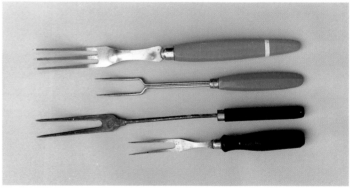

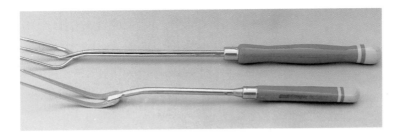

A&J produced both of these unused forks. The 12.5" fork's handle is marked "Chromium Plated." The 15" fork has "Chrome" stamped on its handle. $18-22 each if mint as shown.

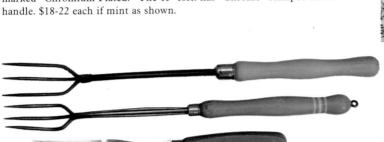

Three wooden handled forks display more variations. The aqua handled fork is 15" long and the green-with-stripes handled fork is 14.25" long. The 10.25" green handled fork is the only one marked. It was produced by Samson and made in the U.S.A. $12-15 each.

Both forks shown have bakelite handles. The two-prong fork is 8" long and marked "Stainless Steel." "AMSILCO" is stamped on the 8.5" four-prong fork. $12-15 each.

"FOLEY FORK MPLS" is marked on this 11" red handled frying fork. These were even made with a pink handle. $12-15.

The paper sleeve for this 10.5" fork states "Quikut Stainless." The handle is marked "Styron." $5-7.

This advertisement for Styron was published in the September 1949 issue of *Ladies' Home Journal.*

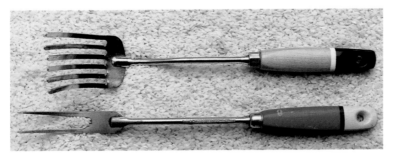

The 11.5" frying fork was manufactured by EKCO. Its handle style is not a popular one. The red, black, and buff fork is 13" long and marked as follows: "Stainless Steel Throughout EKCO ETERNA Stainless Steel Made in U.S.A." Frying fork $5-7, red fork $10-12.

Handy Things Manufacturing Company from Ludington, Michigan, manufactured this "Handy Duplex Serving Fork." Squeezing the handles together closes the prongs thus creating a gripping tool. $15-20.

The red bakelite handled fork is marked "Stainless Steel Made in the U.S.A." $18-22.

French Fry Cutters

In an era of convenience cooking and fast food it is interesting to see the abundance of collectors purchasing french fry cutters to use and not merely for display. Handle colors vary but beyond this fact there are two main differences in cutters. The first is the actual mechanism; the most common french fry cutters have one handle upon which you press down (hard!). The second consideration is whether or not the unit has removable blades. Most cutters have one blade that is permanently attached. Some models do offer removable blades creating size options of the french fries.

If purchasing a french fry cutter for use, examine the metal parts carefully for rust or corrosion. Lift and drop the handle(s) to test ease of motion. Consider which handle design you prefer and whether changing cutting blades is important.

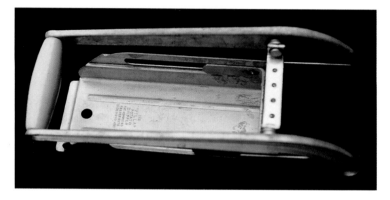

Light blue is a rare color for a french fry cutter. This 9.75" model is "The 'Villi' Potato Chipper" from England. The cutting blades are permanently attached. $18-22.

This is the "EKCO Miracle 2-in-1 Number T-10 French Fry Cutter." The blades change for twenty-five-piece or fifty-piece cutting. $10-15 with box, $18-22 without box.

"Mrs. Damar's Professional Potato Cutter" is unique because the metal is white enamel. The blade is removable but no alternate blades are available. Perhaps this design was for ease when cleaning. $12-18 with box, $7-10 without box.

Made in England, this Nutbrown cutter is almost 10" across when closed and 6.5" tall when open and ready to load. $20-25.

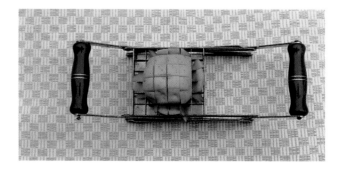

A green handled Nutbrown french fry cutter is a rare find. This view permits easy view of the distinctive silver stripes found on many Nutbrown kitchen gadgets. It is mechanically identical to the red Nutbrown cutter in the following photograph. $20-25.

Garnishing Tools

Garnishing tools allow the cook an opportunity to create a visual display with food presentation. Many useful kitchen gadgets such as peelers, corers, and cutters belong in the category of garnishing tools. Interesting items other than tools were also available to encourage culinary creativity.

Garnishing tools were produced with handles made of metal, plastic, bakelite, and wood. Chances are someone seeking a specific handle treatment to coordinate with a set of kitchen tools will be able to do so.

Most purchasers intend to utilize the item selected so the condition of the metal is important. Stainless steel surfaces provide the most durable, rust-free cutting edges.

"Stainless steel" is embossed on both the metal and wood of this parer and corer. $12-15.

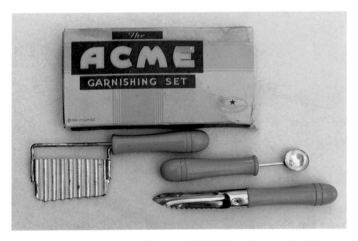

The Acme Garnishing Set is from 1935. This American-made trio advertised that "tastefully served food tastes better" and cost $1.00. The plain green handles are in the original paint. Included are a garnisher, parer and corer, and ball cutter. $15-20 set with box.

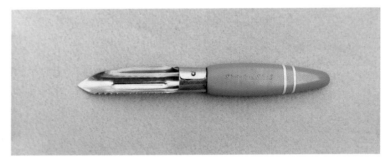

Both the wooden handle and metal cutter of this tool are marked "Stainless Steel." It measures 6.75" in length, was made by A&J, and remains in like-new condition. $12-15 mint.

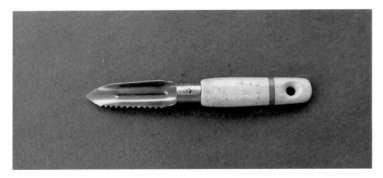

The 6.5" long parer and corer is from A&J. It has stainless steel cutting edges in usable condition. $10-12.

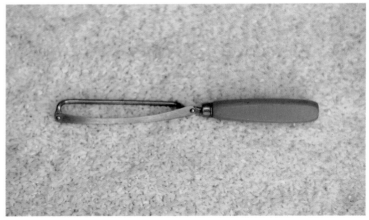

A harder to find item, this 8" long parer is unmarked. $10-15.

The three parer and corer tools have different red, wooden handles. The one on the left and in the center are by A&J and measure just over 6.5". The 7" "bullet" handled parer and corer was manufactured by Androck. $10-12 A&J (if perfect), $7-10 Androck.

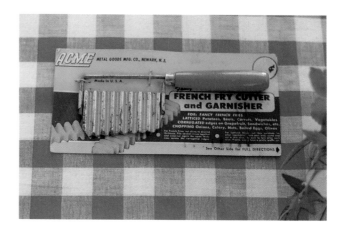

Marketed as a "Fancy French Fry Cutter and Garnisher," Acme Metal Goods Mfg. Co., Newark, New Jersey, produced this 6.5" long gadget. $12-15 (without cardboard $5-7).

All three parers have different handles and overall designs. The green bakelite handled parer and corer on the left measures 6.25" and is unmarked. This is a rarely found kitchen tool. Household Specialties Co. from Union, New Jersey, produced the potato peeler in the center. It is 6" long. The original 25 cent price is still visible on the 6.75" EKCO ETERNA parer and corer on the right. Bakelite (left) $30-35, peeler (center) $7-10 (without cardboard $5-7), parer and corer (right) $10-12.

This red handled garnisher is just over 6.5" in length. $5-7.

S&S Devault patented this parer-grater combination in 1938. It is 5" long and 2" wide. Although it is a uniquely clever tool, few people add it to their collections due to the lack of a colored handle. $5-7.

Here are two unmarked garnishers with green wooden handles. $5-7 each.

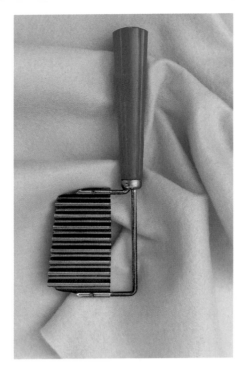

The blade of this bakelite handled garnisher is marked "Stainless." It is almost 7.25" long. $25-30.

With a 7" blade this garnisher provides the largest cutting surface of the examples presented. HUOT from St. Paul manufactured this with a plastic handle and a design that will allow for easy chopping. $7-10.

John Clark Brown, Inc. produced this chopper in 1956. Two prices, 15 cents and 29 cents, appear on the 4 x 7.25" cardboard. With cardboard $12-15, without cardboard $3-5.

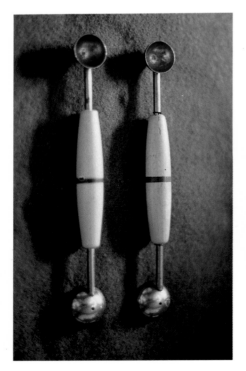

The melon ball cutter on the top is A&J and the one on the bottom is A&J EKCO. Both are 7.75" long. $7-10 each.

This green handled melon ball cutter is 5.5" long and unmarked. $10-12.

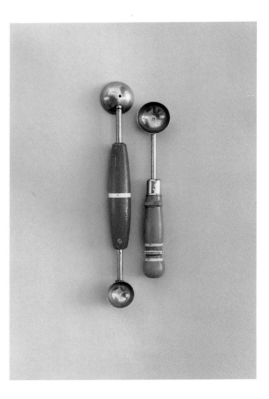

The unmarked green handled cutter is almost 6" long. A&J made the red handled melon ball cutter that is just over 7.5" in length. $7-10 each.

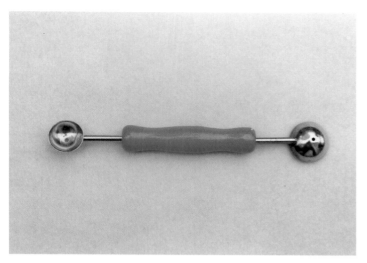

This red handled melon ball cutter is 7.5" long. $7-10.

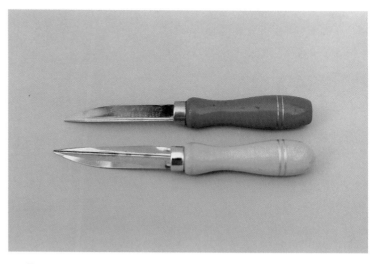

Two silver stripes on the handles indicate a Nutbrown gadget from England. These 6.5" fruit decorators have stainless steel blades. $12-15.

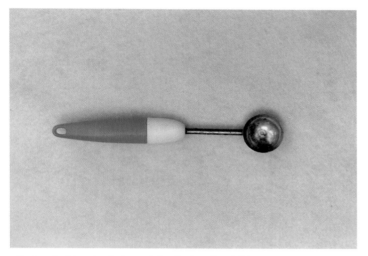

Red and white plastic is used for the handle of this unmarked 6.25" long melon ball cutter. $7-10.

B&B Remembrance from St. Paul created this plastic radish cutter and garnisher. The "Lil Chef" is 5.5" tall and 3.5" wide. $10-15.

The original price of 50 cents is on an end flap of this Aerflo Rotary Slicer. Strictly a garnishing tool, the box promises that it "makes each dish you serve a work of art." Lack of a colored handle reduces the collectibility of this item. With box $8-10, without box $3-5.

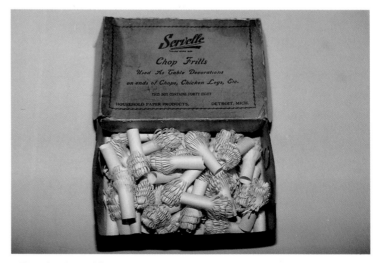

Here is a box of forty-eight "Chop Frills Used As Table Decorations on ends of Chops, Chicken Legs, Etc." The 2.25" long paper frills are from Household Paper Products, Detroit, Michigan. $18-22 box and contents.

From England comes the "Tala Icing Set for the successful hostess." It contains one 6" syringe and six tips. $12-15 with original box as shown, $3-5 without box.

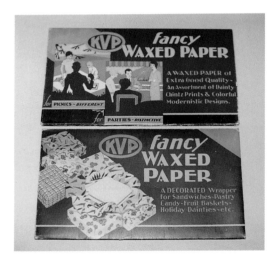

B-Deks, at 39 cents, promised "Decorative food thrills for anniversaries and special occasion cakes." Each bottle contains 1.5 ounces of tinted silvers. $20-25 as packaged.

KVP Fancy Waxed Paper from the Kalamazoo Vegetable Parchment Company in Michigan is dated 1931. The forty piece set was for "table decorations, place doilies, brightening sick rooms trays, for wrapping jellies, confections, and children's lunches." The first picture shows the front and back of the package, and the second picture is an opened package. $20-25

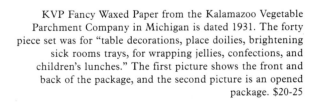

Graters

Graters serve a multitude of purposes, and so they are available in a variety of designs. Some have handles in wood or metal and some have none. Others have curved ends to hang over the sides of a bowl when placed horizontally on top. There are single purpose graters with one shredding surface, double purpose graters with dual textured surfaces, and even a five option model.

Colored, wooden handled graters are the most difficult to find and therefore the most costly. Stainless steel graters will endure use best but just about any grater adds charm when displayed on a kitchen wall. Consider wiring cookie cutters or other gadgets to a grater to create a thematic display.

Remark Manufacturing Company from Butler, Indiana, produced the 4.25 x 11" Simplex grater. $15-20.

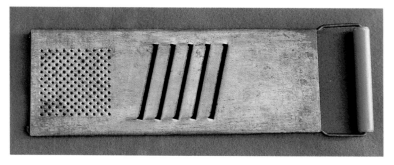

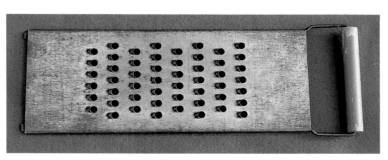

The three green, wooden handled graters are unmarked. Each has a different shredding surface measuring 4.25 x 13". $15-20 each.

Without a colored, wooden handle this 4 x 11" grater will have less value. It was made by Lusher Brothers in Elkhard, Indiana. $5-7.

This 4.25 x 13" grater has two cutting surfaces contributing to its name: "Rapid Slaw and Vegetable Cutters." It is marked "Bluffton Slaw Cutter Co., Bluffton, O." $5-7.

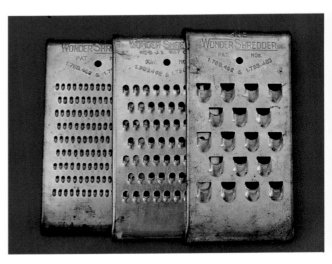

These three Wonder Shredders were designed to nest together. $5-7 each.

A 1930 patent date is on this 4.25 x 8.75" MAGIC grater. $5-7.

Five grating textures are available on this circular model simply marked "PAT PEND." It is 11" long and 7.5" across. $7-10.

The Super Salad Shredders box pictures three graters however four were inside. The 4.25 x 8" graters patented in 1933 have "a copper steel base heavily plated for lifetime use." Remark Mfg. Co. Manufactured and distributed them. $25 set with box, $5-7 each.

The Vitex Safety Grater and Vegetable Juice Extractor originally cost 25 cents. This 4.25 x 7.25" grater is made of a very dark green plastic. $7-10 as packaged, $3-5 without package.

Hidden among a fabulous collection of red and white enamelware rests a red handled grater and cookie cutter. Both are more easily seen in the second picture.

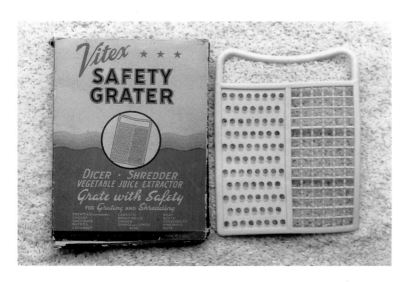

One dollar bought the Vitex Safety Grater in white plastic. Two shredding surfaces are on this 5.25 x 7.25" grater. $7-10 as packaged, $3-5 without package.

Ice Picks

Ice picks were originally used to break blocks of ice into smaller pieces. They sometimes received strong hammer-like blows and so often had protective metal plates at the ends of the wooden handles. There are not many design variations of this simple kitchen tool. Handles are usually one of two styles.

The first is plain or painted wood, and the second is a wooden handle that advertises a business or product. Red is the most common color used, black and green can be found, and other colors present a serious challenge.

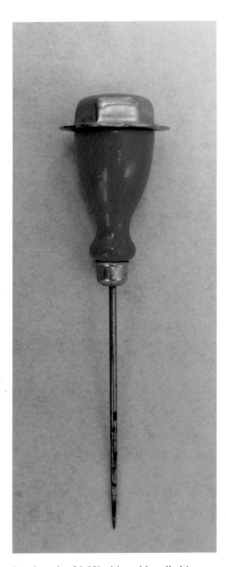

At a length of 8.25", this red handled ice pick is unmarked. $10-12.

Neither of these 8" long ice picks show a manufacturer. The top one advertises Ice Chests and Picnic Jugs from Indiana. Ice picks were often used as promotional pieces. Top $7-10, bottom $12-15.

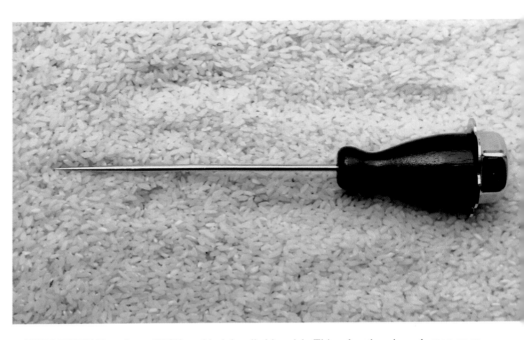

EKCO TAIWAN marks an 8.25" long black handled ice pick. This color, though rarely seen on an ice pick, is one less commonly collected, so is of less value. $10-12.

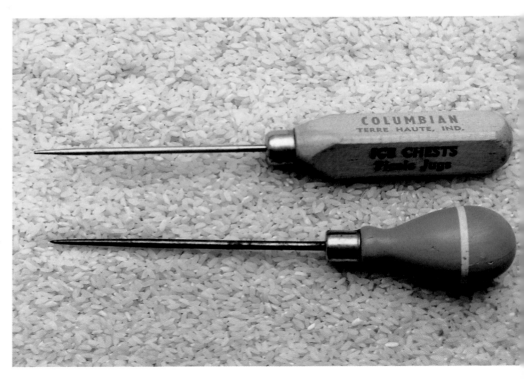

Knives

Whether for cutting, chopping, or spreading, knives are an essential kitchen tool. Since they perform so many tasks they were made in an endless array of styles. Handle treatments and blade sizes and shapes provide a plethora of possibilities. The examples that follow barely represent the realm of knives produced with wood, bakelite, and marbalin handles.

When selecting a knife for purchase determine if it is for display or use. A knife intended to be used must have a blade not only in good condition but securely attached to its handle. Purchase, and then use, the appropriate knife for the job to be done. A knife for display may be selected for handle color and/or style. A picture hanging hook under the blade works nicely when displaying a knife on a wall.

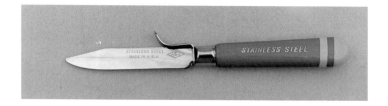

Because knives were used, it is unusual to find one in such pristine condition. A&J made this 6.75" long knife with a stainless steel blade and finger guard. $12-15 mint as shown.

The original stickers are retained on both green wooden handled knives. The knife on top is 10.5" long, and the one below is 6.75" long. $10-12 each.

Utica Superedge sold the "Kitchen Kleaver" for 79 cents. It is 11" long with an "imported rosewood sure-grip handle." $12-15 as packaged, $7-10 without package.

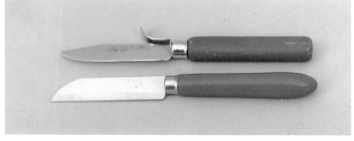

Both American made red wooden handled knives have stainless steel blades, The 6.5" knife on top was by Geneva Forge. Windsor made the knife below. $7-10 each.

Federal Stainless Steel Company in New York produced the "Stainless Steel Carving Set & Pie Server" with "MARBALIN NON-BURN HANDLES.": The knife is 9.75" long. An unused set with original packaging is a special find. $50-60 set as packaged, $10-12 knife or fork, $25-30 pie server.

This bakelite handled grapefruit knife has a stainless steel blade and is 6.75" long. $12-15.

Ladles

In years past a ladle or dipper often hung by the pump, well, or spring. Perhaps it is this history which endears them to many collectors.

The two factors most often considered when making a purchase are color and condition. Ladles are available in many colors and color combinations especially in enamel. This brings us to condition. Enamel collectors usually demand "near mint" pieces. Rust and/or chipped enamel will not only detract from the value of a ladle it may cause it to be unwanted and thus virtually valueless. Wooden handled collectors tend to be less fussy. They seem delighted to locate a handle design that matches their other gadgets.

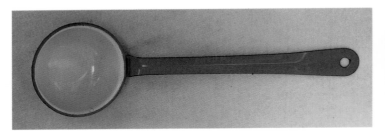

This 14" red and white enamel ladle is in "near mint" condition. Other color combinations may include (but are not limited to) black and white, blue and white, buff and red, and green and yellow. $15-25 near mint.

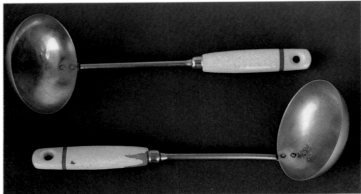

Two identical unmarked 12" ladles are in different condition. $10-12 top, $5-7 bottom.

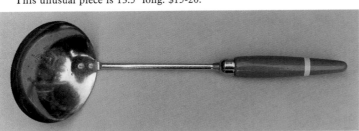

The black wooden handle of this ladle is attached to an aluminum bowl. This unusual piece is 13.5" long. $15-20.

Blue handled kitchen gadgets are hard to find, especially in such great condition. This 12" long ladle is unmarked. $15-18.

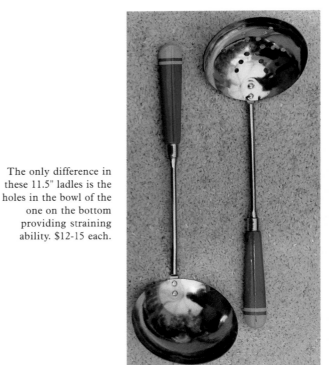

The only difference in these 11.5" ladles is the holes in the bowl of the one on the bottom providing straining ability. $12-15 each.

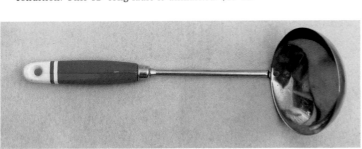

EKCO manufactured this 11.25" long red handled ladle. $10-12.

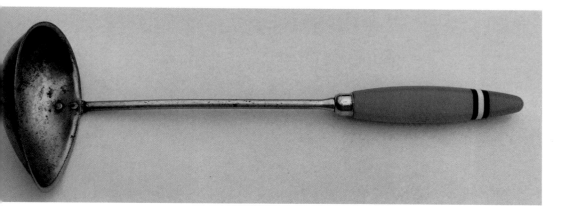

At 12.5" in length this A&J ladle is designed for easy pouring. (Look at "Spoons" for another ladle such as this and the previous one.) $10-12.

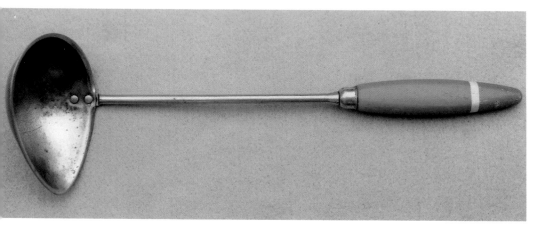

This 13" green handled ladle is from A&J. $12-15.

Both red bakelite handled ladles were made in the United States and are marked as being stainless steel. The ladle on top was made by Englishtown. This company produced many good quality bakelite handled kitchen gadgets. It is 11.5" long, and the one below is 10.5" long. $20-25 each.

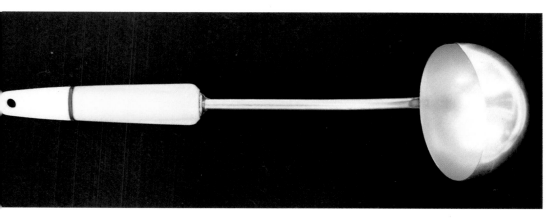

"Stainless Steel Throughout" is embossed on the shaft of this 11.5" long ladle with a yellow and white plastic handle. $12-15.

Match Safes

In a kitchen with a wood burning or gas stove a match safe was basic equipment. The purpose of a match safe is just as its name indicates, to keep the house, its contents, and its inhabitants safe while providing an accessible storage facility for matches.

Early match safe designs were basic and utilitarian. Many were advertising items that now have a high level of collectibility and a commensurate price. As canister sets and other decorative metal items became common, kitchen accessories with matching pieces were inevitable. Match safes were one of many products metalware manufacturers created to accompany their canisters, trash cans, bread boxes, etc.

Purchase of a match safe is usually based on finding one that is part of a metalware set being collected. Because match safes are hard to locate many collectors are more forgiving of their condition than of any other metal kitchen decorations.

Dimensions are very similar as each match safe had to store a standard box of wooden matches. For this reason measurements will not be included in this section.

The functional design of an early match safe is evident in this "Safe Home Match Holder." $50-60.

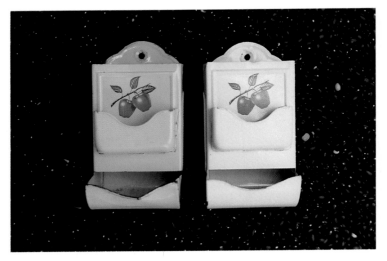

"Made in USA" is stamped on both apple match safes. The yellow safe on the left has a 20 cent price stamped on the back. $45-50 each.

This "Lady at the Gate" match safe shares the same mold design as the last two flowers. Its condition shows wear but this graphic is more difficult to locate than florals. $20-25 as shown, $50-60 if mint.

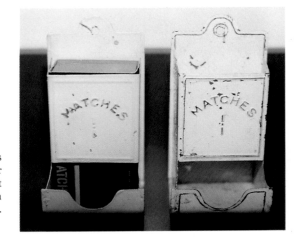

This pair of match safes indicates a bit more concern for aesthetics. The safe on the left sports a touch of red, but both are still quite plain. $20-25 each.

Each of the following five match safes is unmarked. The first three flowers
and the last two flowers appear to share common molds. $40-45 each.

Meat Tenderizers

Collections may be based on a color. Collections may be based on an item. If there are any meat tenderizer collectors, I haven't met you yet!

Meat tenderizers are not a significantly popular item like cookie cutters and potato mashers, but they have been produced in an interesting assortment of designs. Perhaps this brief presentation will spark some interest in this neglected gadget.

An original sticker remains on a green handled Munising Quality Meat Tenderizer. Almost 11.25" long, it was produced by Munising Wood Products Co. in Munising, Michigan. $18-20.

This 11.25" long green handled meat tenderizer is unmarked. $15-18.

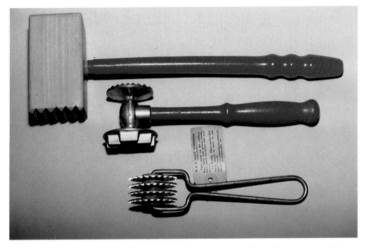

Here are three totally different meat tenderizers. The all wood model on top is 13.25" long from Yugoslavia. Modern Industries in Des Moines produced the 9" wood and aluminum tenderizer in the center. The 7.5" "B&H Meat Tenderer" was made in Shoemakersville, Pennsylvania. It retains an original tag. $15-18 each.

EKCO Products Company in Chicago manufactured the Mary Ann Meat Tenderizer. It is 10.75" long and has the original packaging around its "durable northern hardwood." $20-25 as packaged.

The 1.75 x 1.5 x 3.25" Butcher Block Meat tenderizer from Japan makes the following claim: "Makes any cut of meat tender, tasty, and easily digestible. 48 sharp stainless steel blades with hardwood handle." $18-20 with box.

Openers

Openers are a showcase of human ingenuity. Bottles, cans, and jars require opening, and the assortment of devices created for this task are endless. Many are so multipurpose and versatile they become almost too complex to use. Others are so simple and dependable they may be found in a kitchen still being utilized.

Collectors may select an opener simply because of its uniqueness. They may remember a particular model in grandma's house. Some collectors want a handle treatment that matches gadgets already owned. Consider condition and design when buying an opener. Some of the more uncommon items will command a higher price. Original packages and labels will also augment cost.

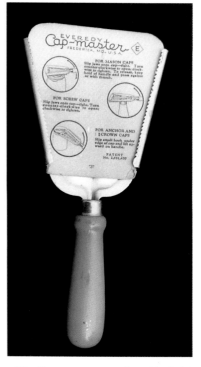

The Cap-master comes from Frederick, Maryland, and is almost 8.25" long. Its design allows for easy gripping of jar and bottle caps that screw on and off. $20-25.

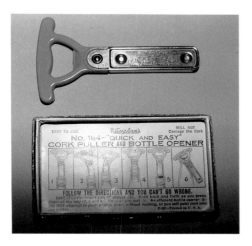

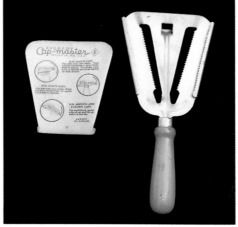

Vaughan's No. 164 "Quick and Easy" Cork Puller and Bottle Opener is only 4.75" long. The directions for use are printed inside the box. The green handle makes this appealing to collectors of this color. $20-25 with box, $15-18 without box.

Patent number 2000982 from 1935 is on this 8" long opener made in the United States. It opens bottles, jars, and cans and probably provides other services as well. $10-15.

An 8" long Grip-all promises it "opens and closes all sizes." Not only does it have a popular green handle, it advertises "Unifil the perfect insulator sold by Grogan-Robinson Lumber Co." Advertisement collectors may also enjoy this gadget. $20-25.

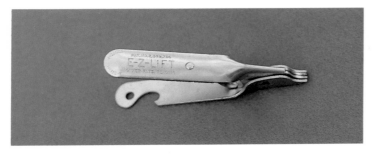

Stewart patented the E-Z-LIFT in 1936 to lift off jar and bottle caps. It is 5" long. $5-7.

No manufacturer is shown on this 8.25" long jar opener that was patented in 1935. $7-10.

This Spear-Cap "opens and re-seals your milk." The aluminum cap has a spear-like protrusion on the other side to break the seal on a milk bottle. It is just over 2.5" across and .5" deep. $5-7.

Before 1925 can openers were awkward and challenging to use. H.J. Edlund invented a usable, practical institutional can opener in 1925 and began the Edlund Company in Burlington, Vermont. His household model was named "Edlund Jr." Pictured are several of his openers. The red handled openers have patent dates "Apr. 21 - May 12 '25 June 18 '29." They are available in a variety of colors.

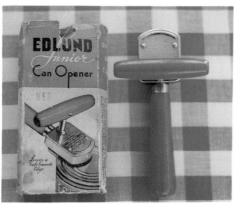

$18-22 with the box.

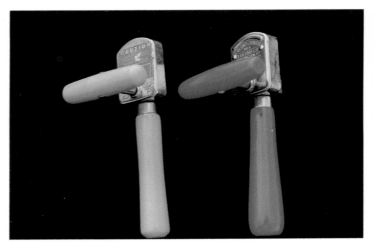

$12-15 each.

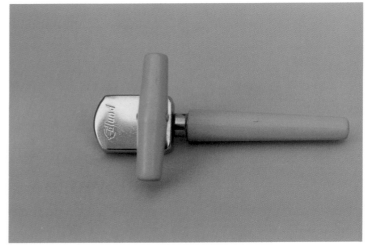

$10-12.

Different companies manufactured can openers with a puncture mechanism. Here are variations of color, handle treatment, and mechanical design.

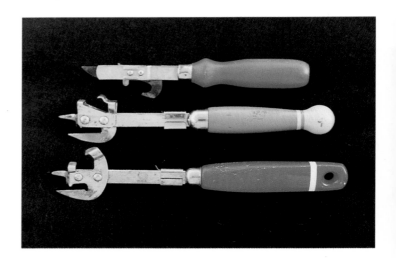

ACME MGM Co. Made the red handled opener on top. It is almost 7" long and is marked "Tempered Tool Steel Blade." The green handled opener in the center is by A&J and measures 8.25" in length. This opener and the 8.75" long opener on the bottom are marked "Tool Steel Tempered." The bottom one is from EKCO. $8-10 red handled, $12-15 green handled.

EKCO made this 7" long opener with a red and white wooden handle. $8-10.

At 8.25" in length this yellow and green handled opener is marked "EKCO A&J USA Tool Steel Tempered." $5-7 as shown with wear.

A&J's almost 8.25" long green handled opener is marked "Tool Steel Tempered." $12-15.

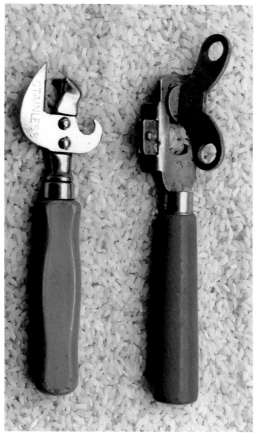

The Taplin Mfg. Co. from New Britain, Connecticut, patented the red handled opener on top in 1936. Both examples are 6" long. The green handled puncture-type opener on the left is simply marked "stainless." $8-10 each.

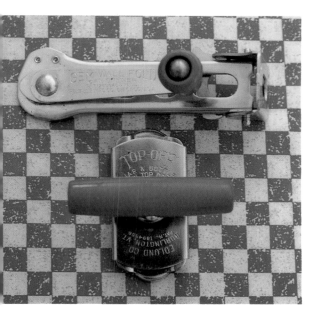

Reliable Manufacturing Co. in Chicago patented the Gem Wall Fold Can Opener pictured on top. It extends 5.5" from a wall when mounted. The Top-Off Jar and Bottle Screw Top Opener changes from less than 1.25" up to 4.25" in not quite one complete rotation of its handle. $12-15 Gem Wall model (top), $7-10 jar opener (bottom).

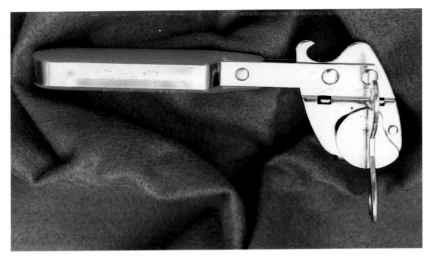

Vaughan's No. 174 Utility Safety Roll is 6" long. Because the red handle is plastic this opener is less collectible even though it has an interesting, complex mechanism. It was made in the U.S.A. $5-7.

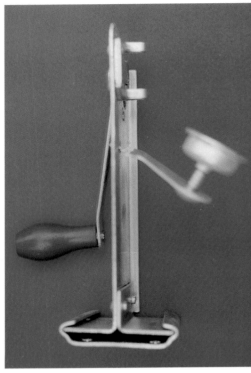

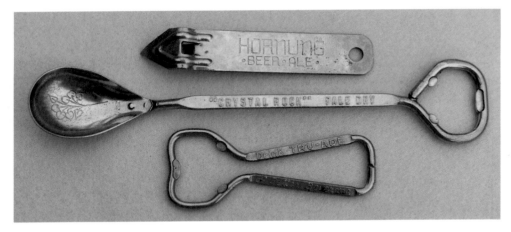

Here are three simple all-metal advertising openers. The Hornung piece on top is a Vaughan item that measures 4" in length. **Advertising items vary tremendously in value depending on the business or company being promoted.** A spoon-opener combination is on the "Crystal Rock" Pale Dry Made in U.S.A. 8" long piece. The opener on the bottom reads "Drink TRU-ADE A Better Beverage." It is 3.5" long. $3-5 each (other advertising pieces can command much higher prices).

The Kitchen Mascot Magnet Can Opener extends 5.75" from the wall and has a blue handle. There are no markings on the opener, but the box states "Made in Japan." $18-20 with box, $10-12 without box.

A November patent date is cut off due to a circle machined into the metal as part of this opener's design. Edlund produced this 4.5" long advertising opener. $7-10 as shown, other companies or businesses can warrant much higher prices.

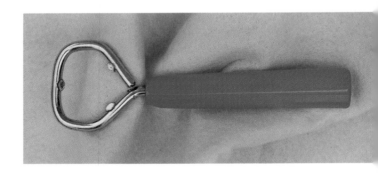

Bakelite was used for many kitchen gadgets, but a bakelite handled bottle opener is uncommon. This piece is 5" long. $25-30.

Plastic

The use of hard plastic as a material in the kitchen was introduced in the late 1940s so these colorful and creative paraphernalia are consider a "fifties thing." Plastic kitchen items are becoming one of the most popular collectibles in the marketplace. The variety of unique tools and gadgets molded from bold, cheerful colors has a mass appeal.

Throughout this book are examples of plastic kitchenware, however this section provides an eclectic look that touches the range of colors. Think of this presentation as the appetizer from an impressive menu of options.

When purchasing hard plastic examine the merchandise carefully for chips and hard-to-notice cracks. Select pieces with good shine and original paint if applicable. Wash these treasures by hand avoiding abrasive detergents and scrubbing materials.

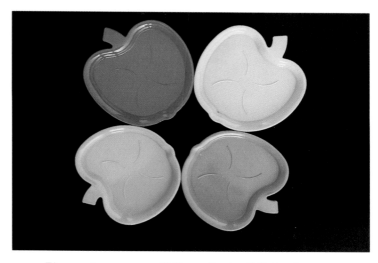

These apple coasters are "A Rogers Product." $2-4 each.

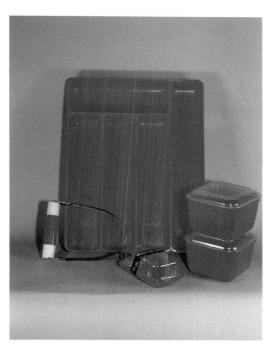

This arrangement offers an array of plastic kitchen items. The Lustro-ware silverware tray is from Columbus Plastic Products Inc., Columbus, Ohio. The quarter pound Burrite Ware butter dish was featured earlier in this book. Columbus Plastic Products Inc. also made the 4 x 4" refrigerator dishes. The dough blender is an Androck item. Utensil tray $15-20, butter dish $12-14, refrigerator dishes $7-10 each, dough blender $8-10.

The maple leaves are also "A Rogers Product." The green and bronze leaves are marked with the number one, and the yellow and tan leaves are marked with the number two. $5-7 each.

Snack tray coaster designs are colorful and carried. Many carry warnings that they are not for use as an ashtray. Here are four of the countless possibilities.

Delagar made the plastic fish dishes. They are 5.5" long and 4.75" wide. $5-7 each.

Both pairs of shakers have hand painted detailing so care must be taken to preserve their look. Niagara Falls is unmarked, the lamp simply has "Pat. Pend." These types of shakers are common and of relatively low value. $5-7 each pair.

An original label remains on one of these "snac-kosters" by Hofmann Industries, Inc. from Sinking Spring, Pennsylvania. The two-part design was intended to hold a snack and cradle a beverage. $5-7 each.

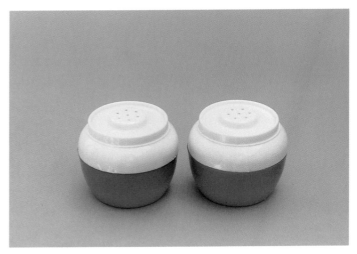

Two inches tall, these unmarked shakers screw apart between the white and green for filling. $10-12.

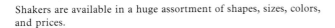

Shakers are available in a huge assortment of shapes, sizes, colors, and prices.

The pair of birds, as shown, is quite rare. The eggs are actually salt and pepper shakers, the eyes are red rhinestones. Most often the eyes are missing or the eggs are lost. Complete, this pair from Radferm, New York, creates a whimsical delight. $25-30.

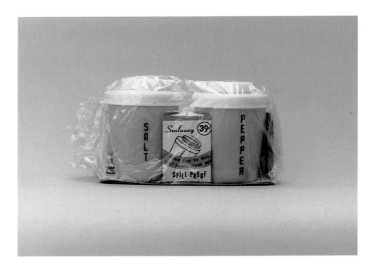

Thirty-nine cents purchased the Sealaway Spill-Proof shaker set. Plastray Corporation from Detroit, Michigan, manufactured this turquoise set available in pink and gray, too. $15-18 as packaged, $8-10 without package.

The letters "P" and "S" are formed by the pouring holes of these unmarked flower buds. This method of demarcation was often used on plastic shakers. $8-10.

Plas-Tex from Los Angeles patented this hard to find flour shaker. It is 4.5" tall. $15-20.

Here are two condiment designs.

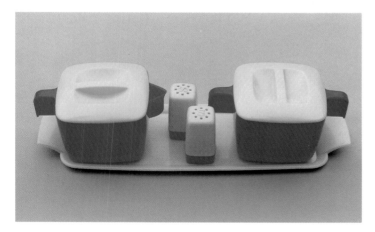

Pieces of this Federal Tool Corp. Chicago, U.S.A. condiment set are common. Finding a complete set may be difficult. Examining this picture carefully will reveal that this set actually has two salts rather than a pepper and a salt. $15-20 for complete correct set.

The tomato condiment has matching shakers. This is unmarked, 2.75" tall, and includes the spoon. Vegetables and fruit have reemerged as decorating themes so tomato accessories are again popular. $12-15 condiment (shown), $12-15 salt and pepper (not shown).

Measuring devices come in many styles. These two are among the more unique possibilities.

Lustro ware created this rooster wall hanging advertising piece. He holds four measuring spoons: ¼ teaspoon, ½ teaspoon, 1 teaspoon, and 1 tablespoon. Two hooks near the feet can hold keys or pot holders. $25-30.

Each arm of this measure for mixing alcoholic beverages is about 3.5" long and includes the following labels: Half Pony ½ oz., Pony 1 oz., Jigger 1½ oz., and Pair Ponies 2 oz. It was made by H.A. Hennessey Co. Rochester, New York. $10-15.

These egg timers include the warning "Do not use for ash tray." They are 5.75" tall and 4" across and manufactured by Plastica, North Wales, Pennsylvania. $16-20

Variety in color and design are evident in this sample of spoon rests.

Pink is a color less commonly used in plastic creations. Amiration's 5" by 5" spoon rest sports a bird motif. $12-15.

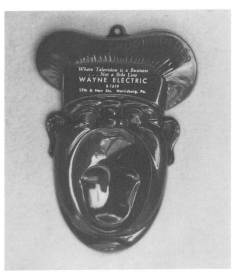

Note the five digit phone number on this advertising spoon rest. The chef is 5.75" long and 4" wide. $15-18.

The three chef spoon rests are identical other than markings on back. The red one is marked "1 U.S.A.", orange is unmarked, and yellow "U.S.A.2". They are 6.5" long and 5" wide. Although orange is the least common of the three, its condition will diminish its value. Red & yellow $8-10 if mint, orange $10-12 if mint.

Hofmann Industries Inc. Sinking Spring, Pennsylvania, produced the No. 97 Salad Bowl with four accompanying bowls and a serving fork and spoon. $10-15 complete set as shown.

Other than MATCHES on the front there are no markings on this yellow match safe. $20-25.

The Burrough Co. from Los Angeles manufactured these Burrite 123 deco pitchers in red as well as yellow and green. Their strong deco styling and flip-up lids make them popular items. $20-25 each.

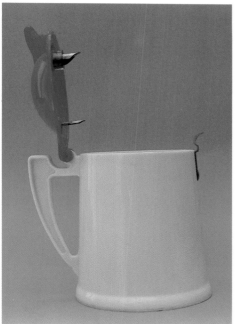

The base of this ice bucket is marked "Brrr! Trade Mark Patents Pending Brrr, Inc. New York, N.Y." It is 7.5" tall with a 7.5" opening. $25-30.

Here are condensed milk pitchers. They have a two-cup capacity and dual piercing blades to open a can as the lid is closed. These are less common items. $20-25.

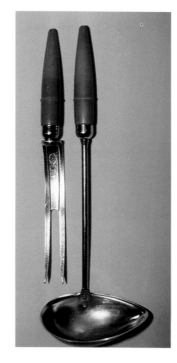

A&J moved into gadget production with plastic handles. The meat fork is 10.5" long, and the ladle is 13" long. $8-10 each.

A breakfast of cereal and soft boiled eggs could be served easily with this bowl from Century Plastic Co., Hudson, Massachusetts. It is 6.75" across and 1.5" deep. $8-10.

The yellow flower of this "SNAP-A-NAP" napkin dispenser slides down and snaps up for use. An Admiration product, it measures 7" square and 2.75" deep. $40-45.

No manufacturer is shown on this five cup sifter. $15-20.

The Jolly Chef Memo Set remains unused and is in a rarely seen turquoise color. "A Reliance Product" is on the memo pad and pencils. There are two metal hooks for the coordinating pot holders. $30-35.

Sixty-nine cents would pay for Pushbutton Bottle Caps. The National Key Co. Plastics Division in Chicago promised these would "snap on and off with the touch of a button." $15-20 as boxed, $1-1.50 each.

A winking, moustached chef is commonly used in kitchen collectibles. This example has pinkies extended as hooks for hanging pot holders and/or keys. The 5.25" tall wall hanging is "A ROYAL PRODUCT." $15-20.

The plastic 4" x 8" refrigerator dish has a matching 6" x 12.5" tray. Both are unmarked. Refrigerator dish $8-10, tray $5-7.

Wall hangings often served a purpose such as holding keys, plants, or pot holders. This 5.5" long, unmarked hanging's sole job was to be a decoration. $18-20.

These insulated tumblers have an eleven ounce capacity and filigree design. $10-15 set of four.

80

Potato Mashers

Potato mashers are among the most collected of any single kitchen gadget. It may be the memory of delicious homemade mashed potatoes, or the simplicity of design that eases food preparation, but for whatever reason they are actively sought after to hang on walls, store in crocks, use as a base for dried and silk flower arrangements, or make mashed potatoes.

The possibilities are endless. Handle styles vary, color treatments change, and metal fabrications differ.

Wooden handled potato mashers are both the most commonly found and most frequently collected handle treatment. As with other utensils made with wooden handles, look for original paint in good condition. Because these were among the most heavily used kitchen tools the challenge presented to a collector is finding a pristine handle. The examples in this section show a broad range of condition and a vast realm of possibilities. Value is determined by both condition and rarity of design.

Plastic and bakelite were also utilized for potato masher handles. They are less common and yet less desired.

The following section is organized beginning with common and/or worn wooden handles. The quality and value of the handles improves through the presentation. Plastic and bakelite handles follow. Since overall dimensions are fairly similar they are not included.

Expect to pay around $8.00 for any of the following potato mashers.

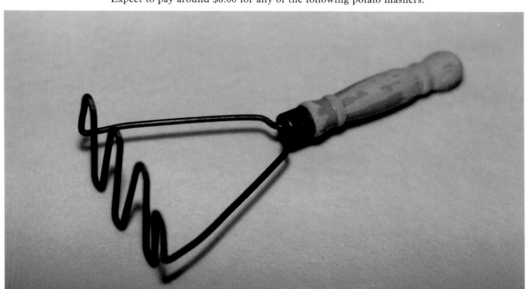

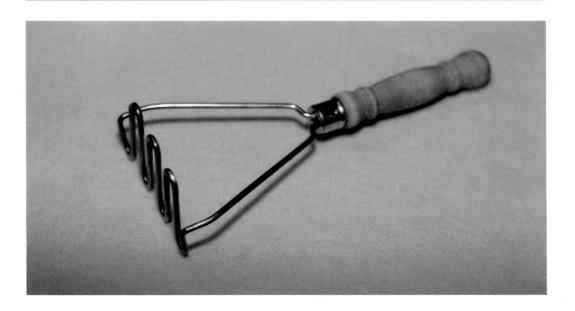

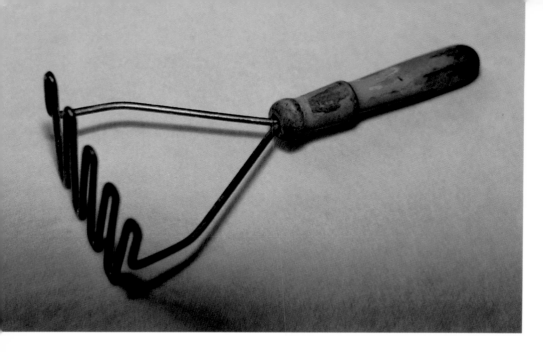

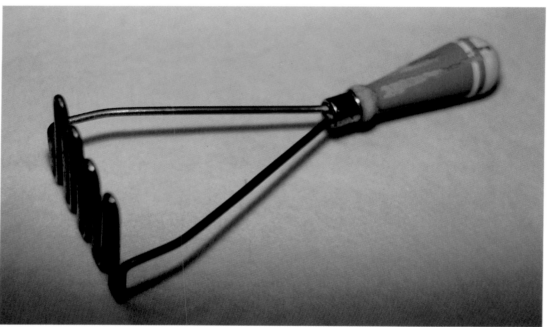

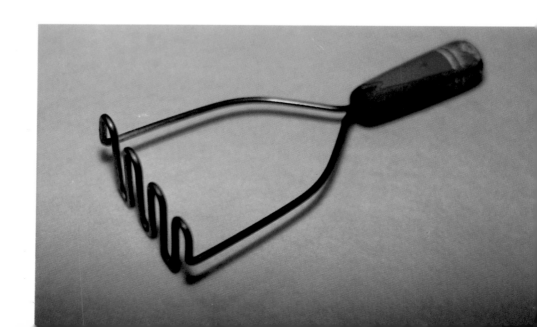

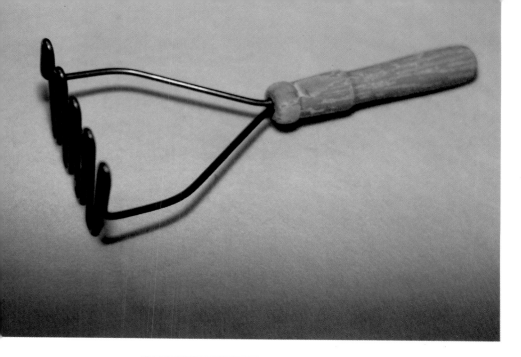

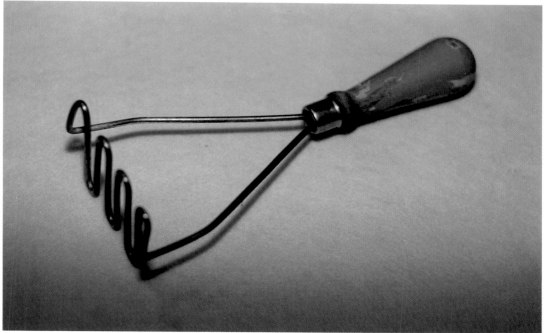

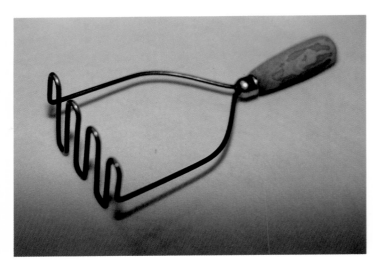

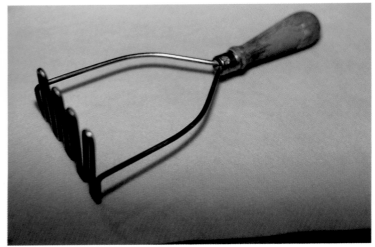

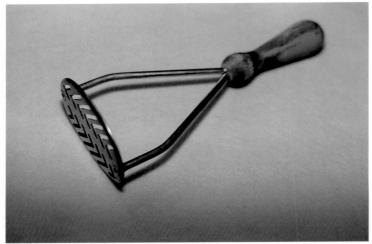

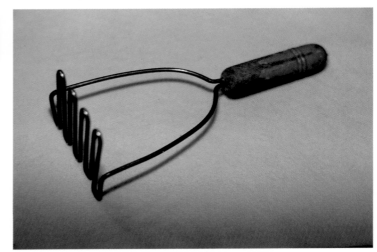

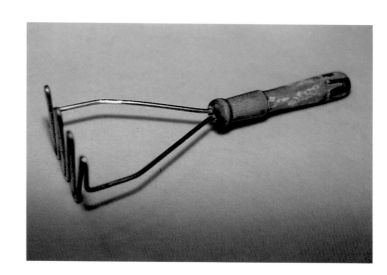

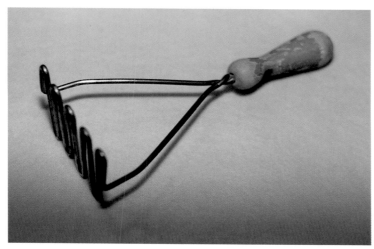

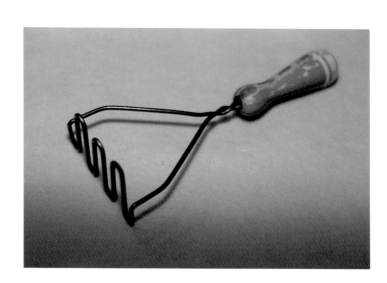

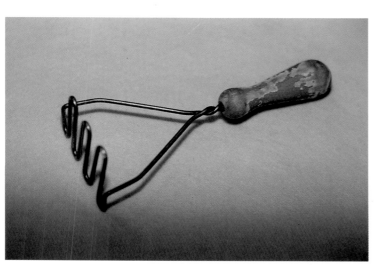

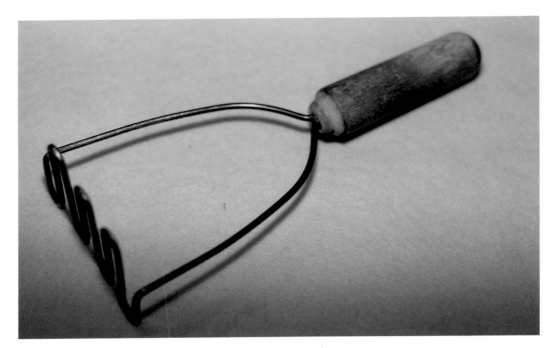

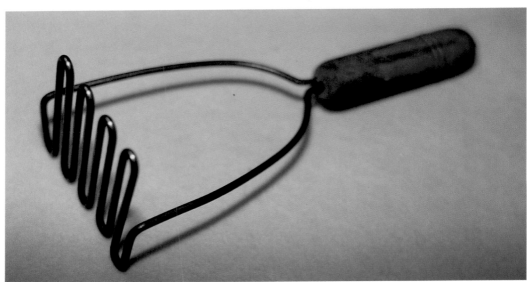

This next group of mashers is valued from $8-10 each.

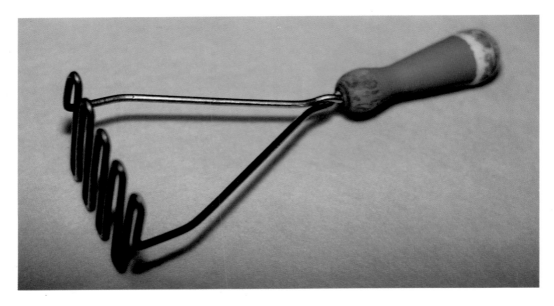

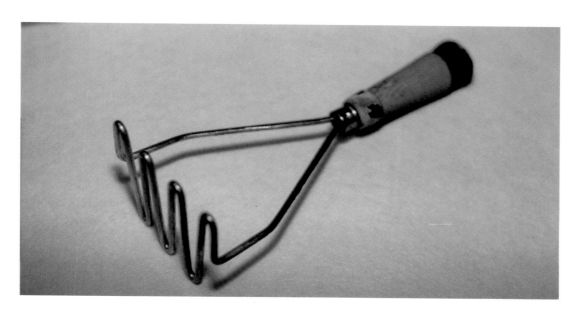

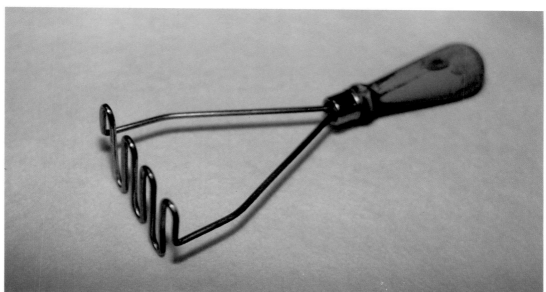

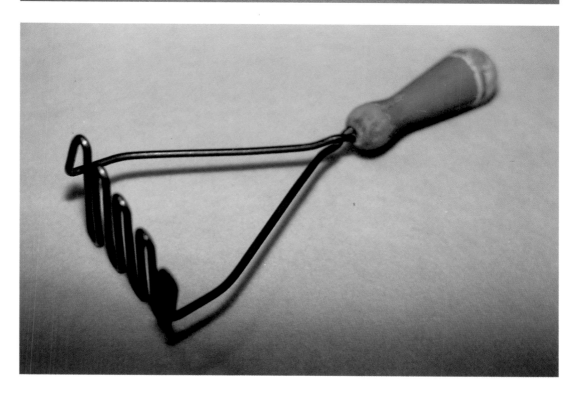

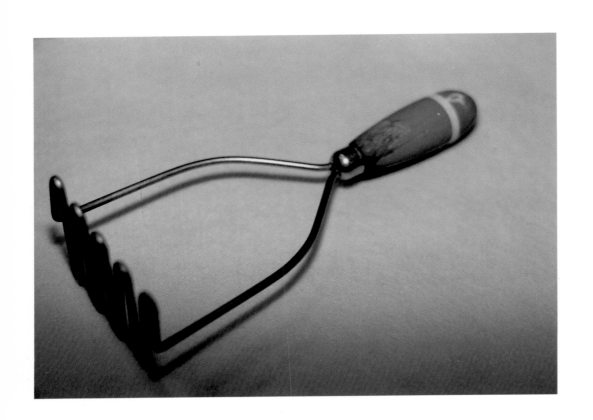

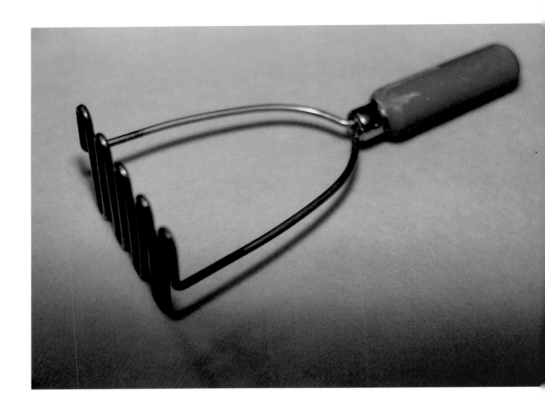

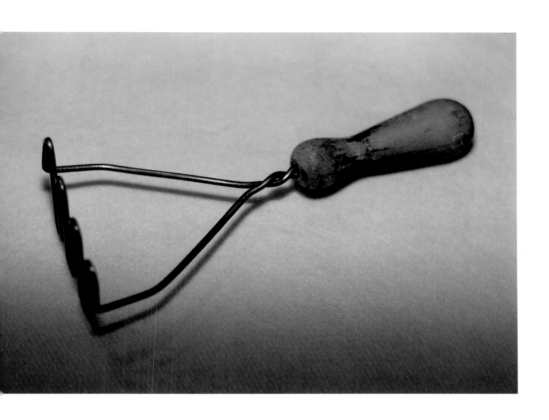

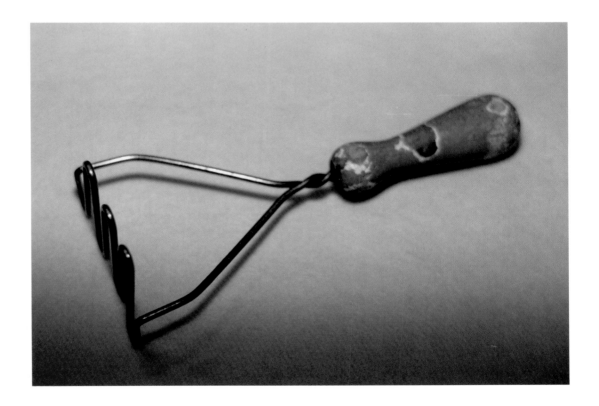

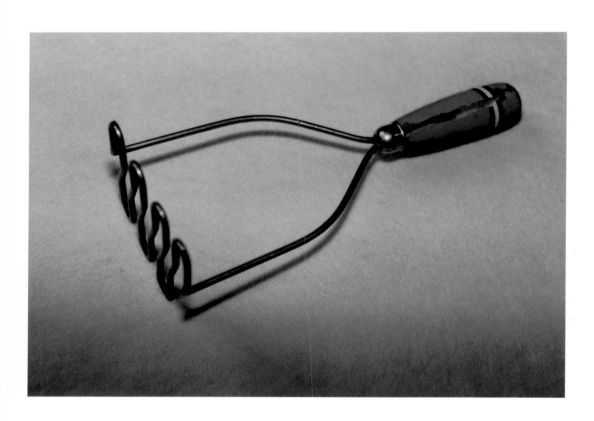

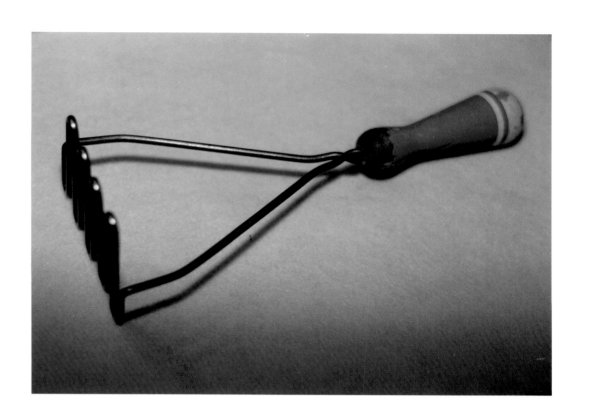

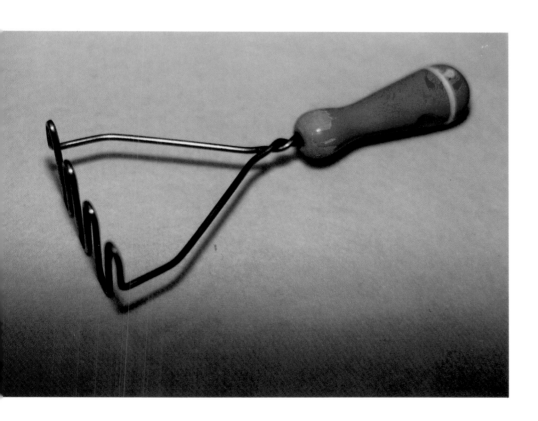

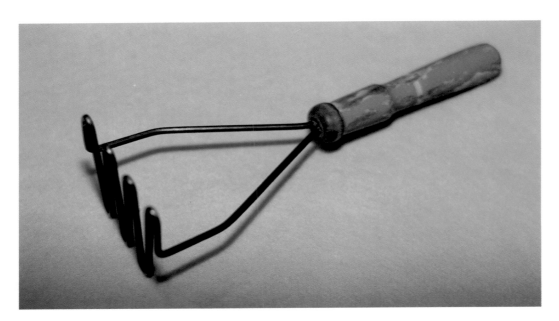

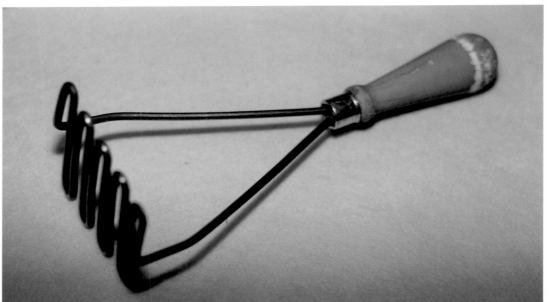

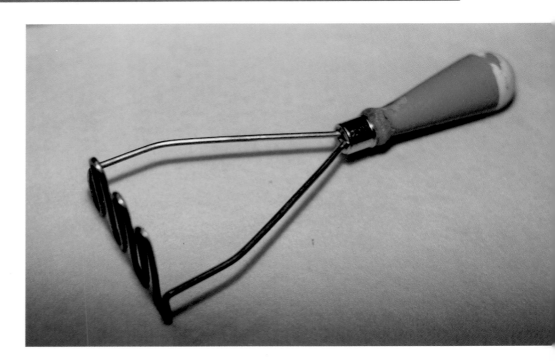

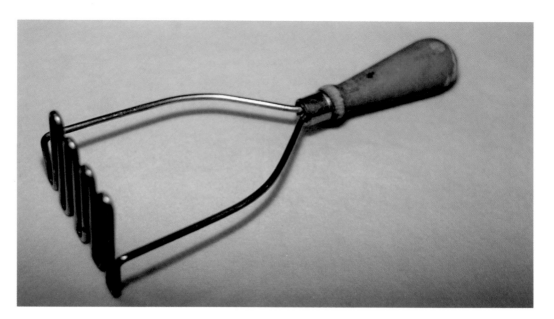

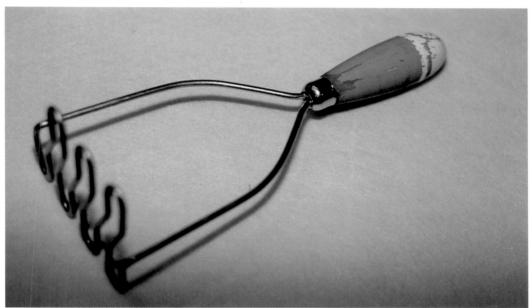

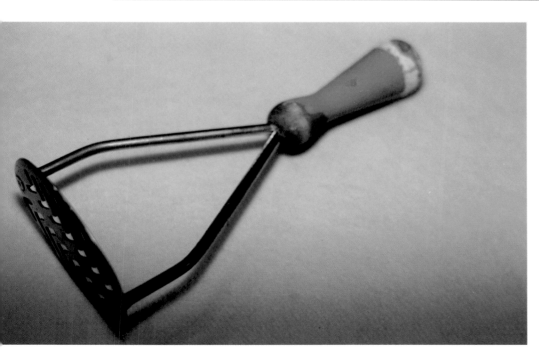

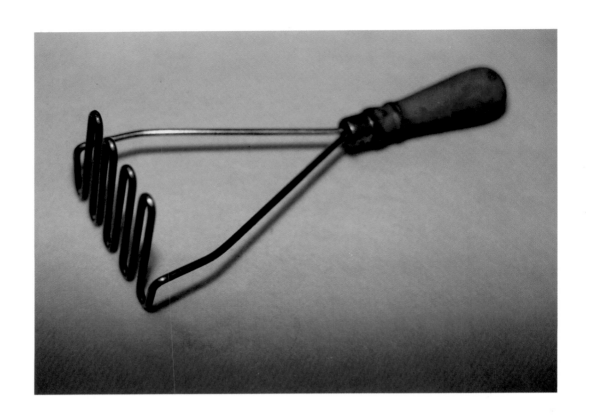

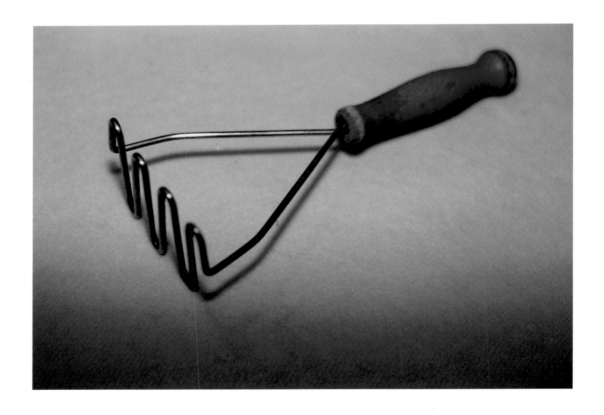

These potato mashers should cost from $12-14 apiece.

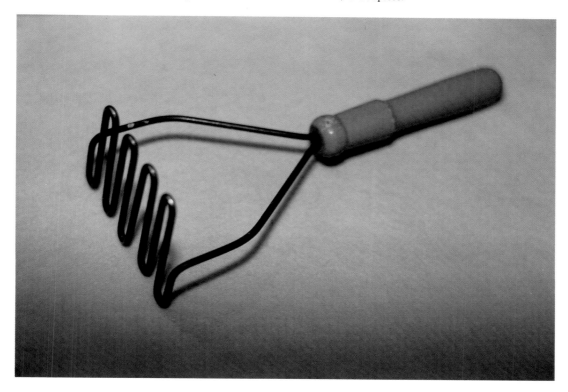

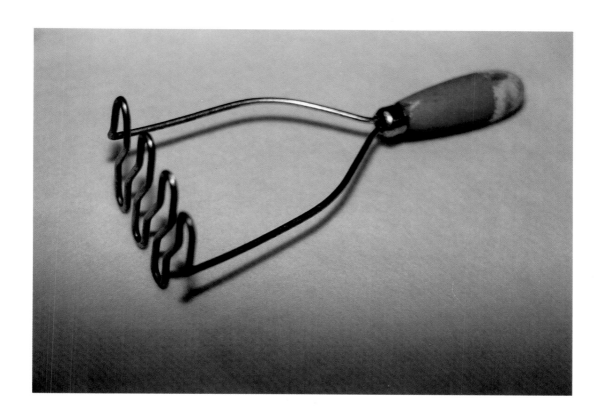

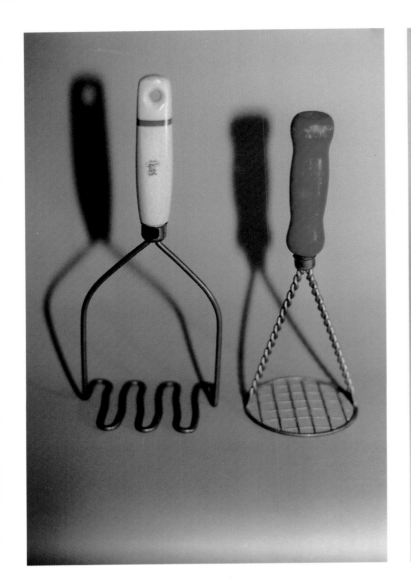

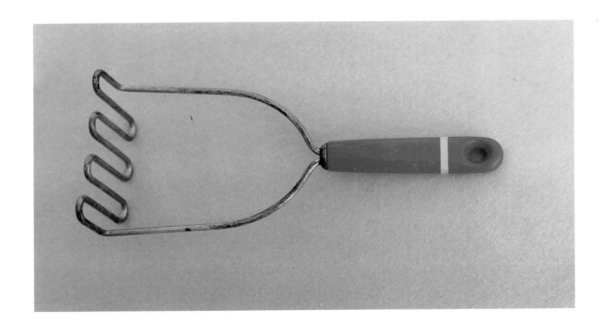

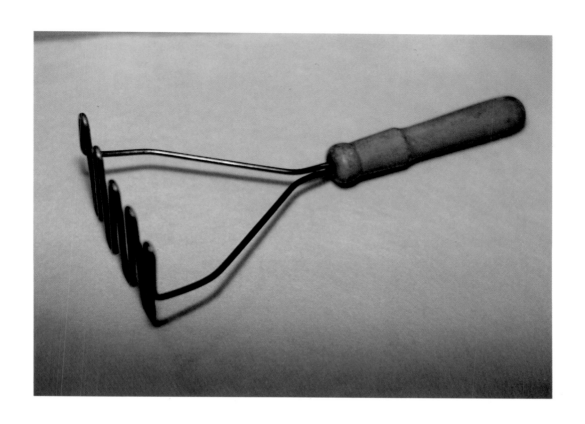

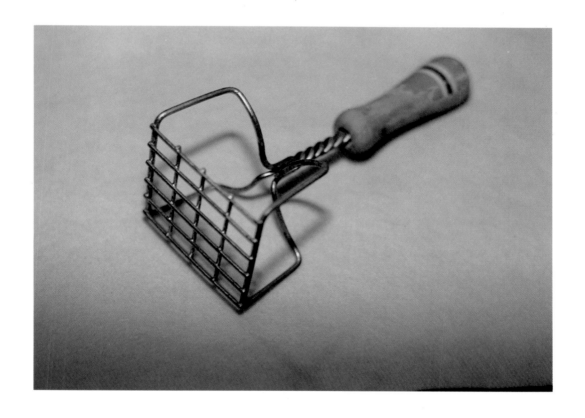

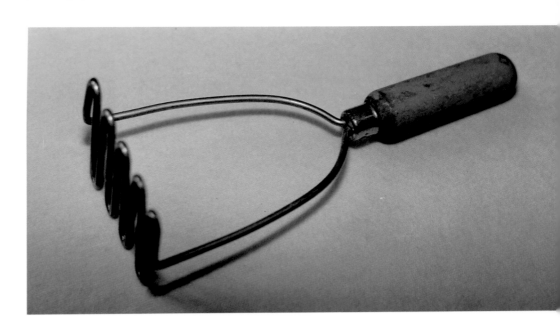

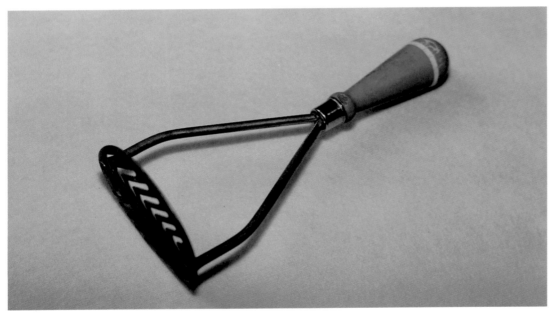

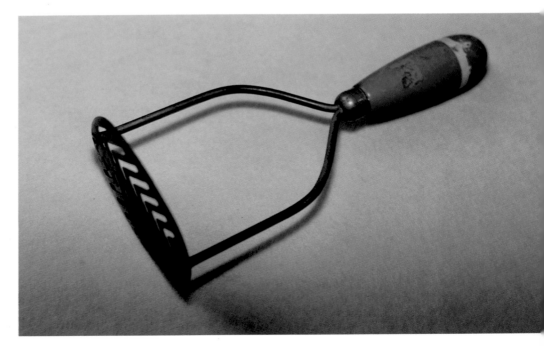

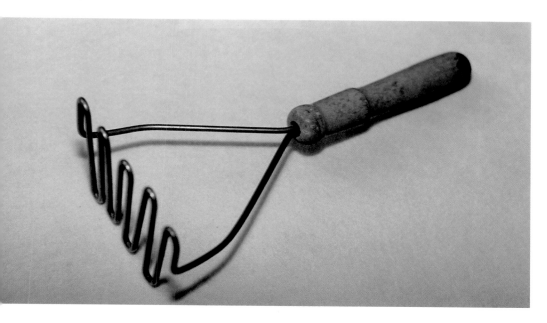

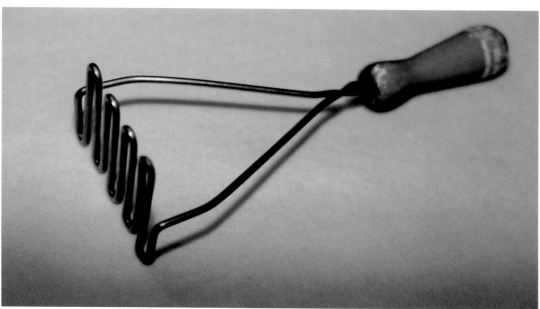

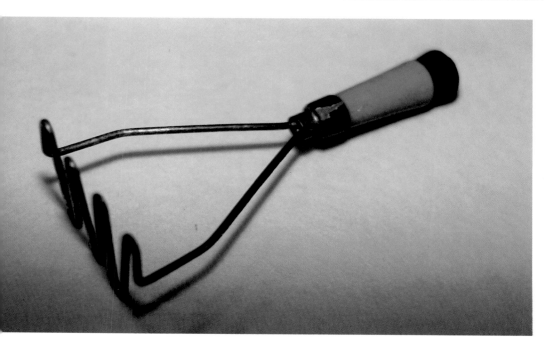

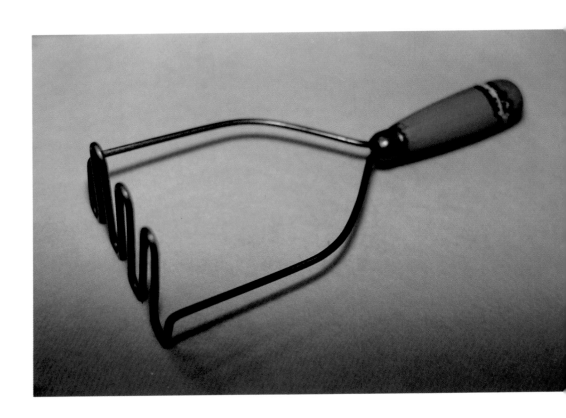

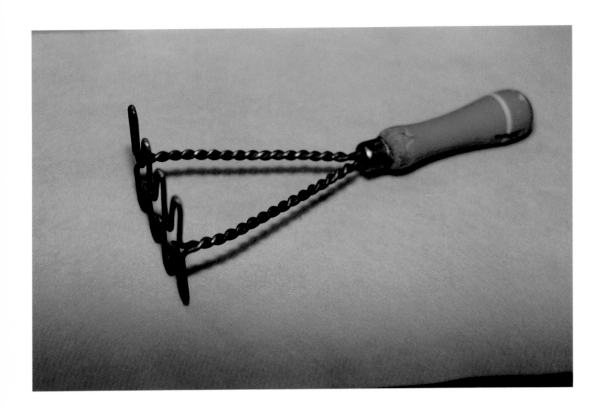

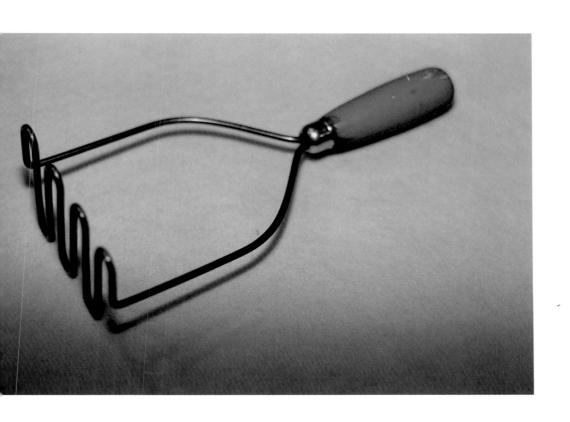

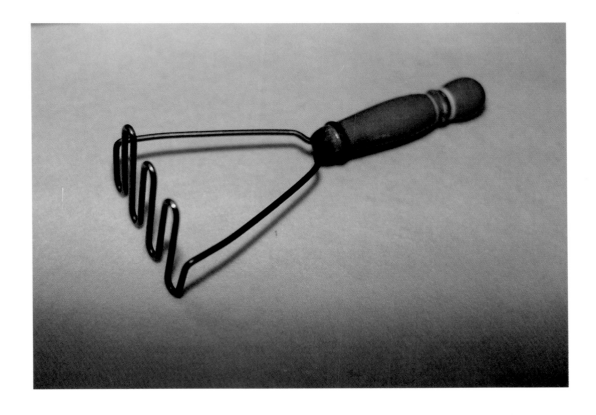

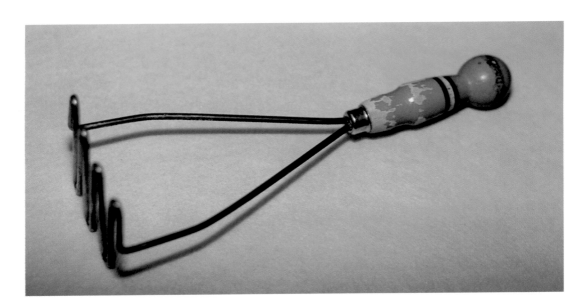

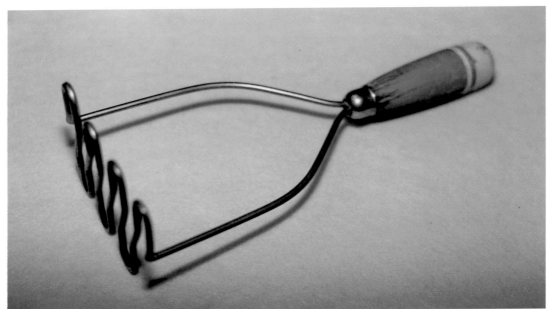

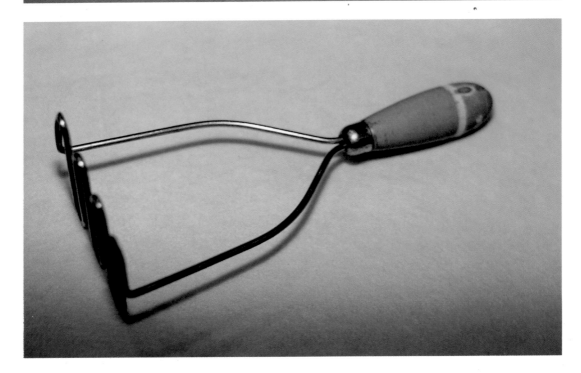

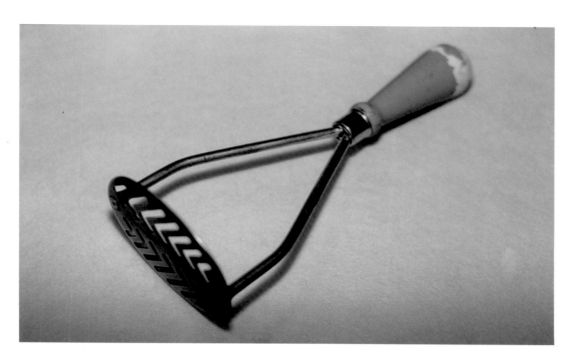

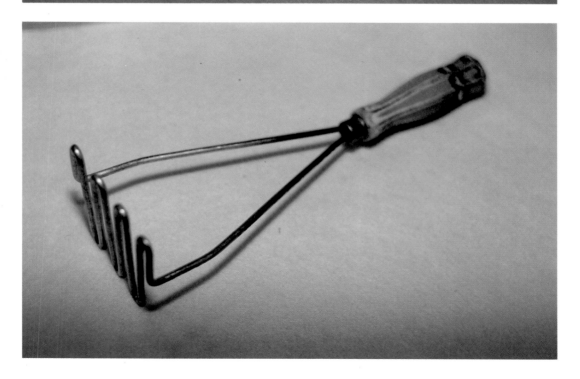

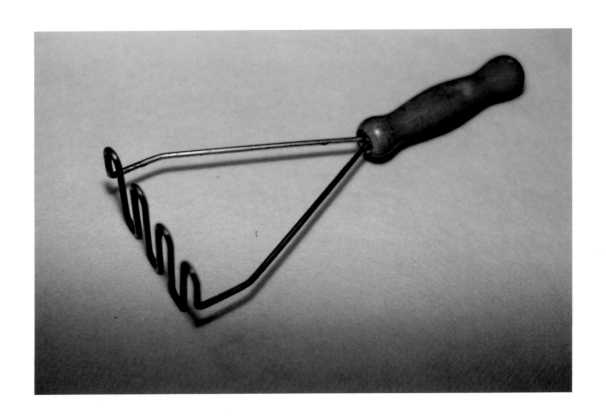

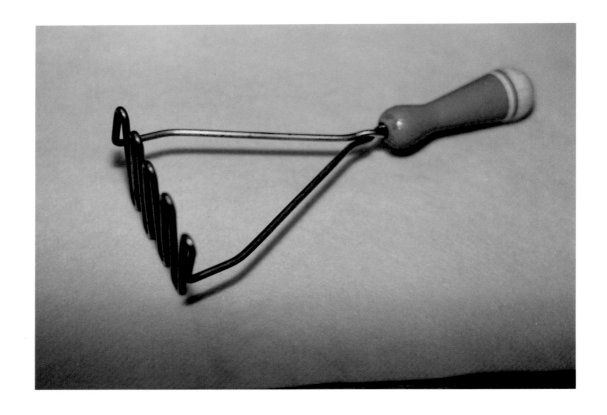

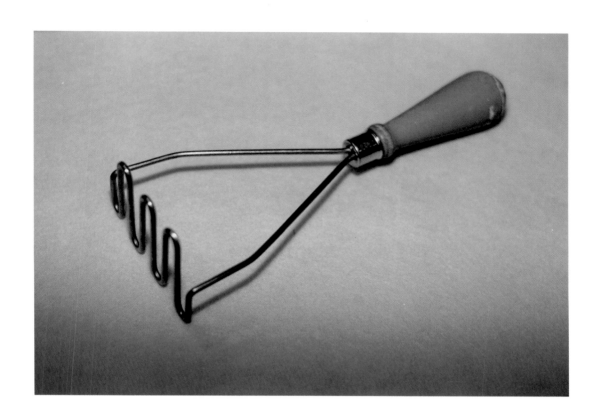

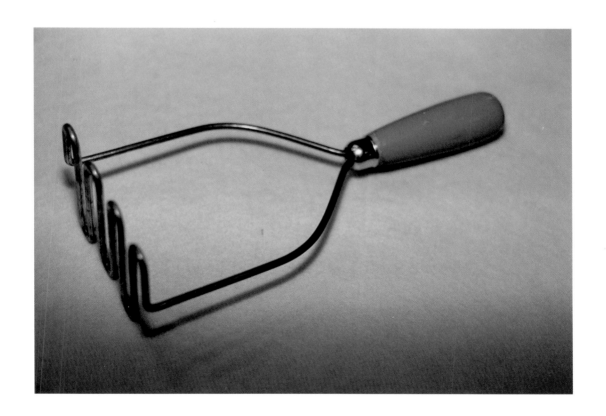

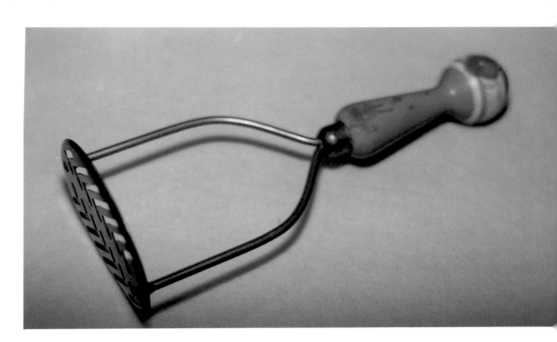

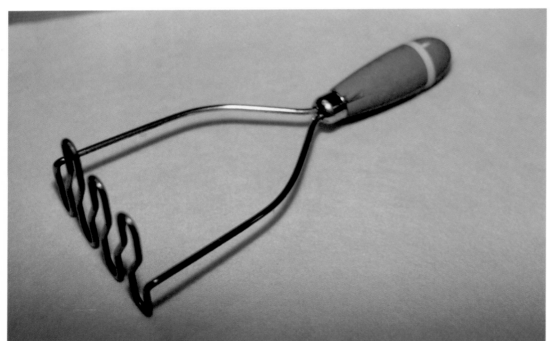

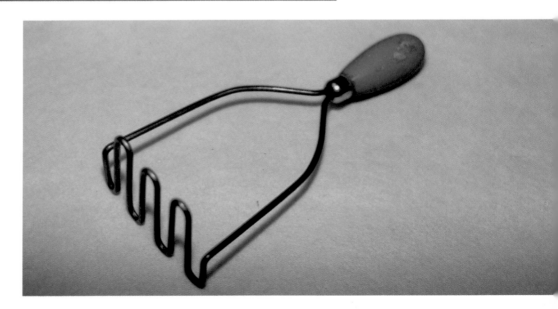

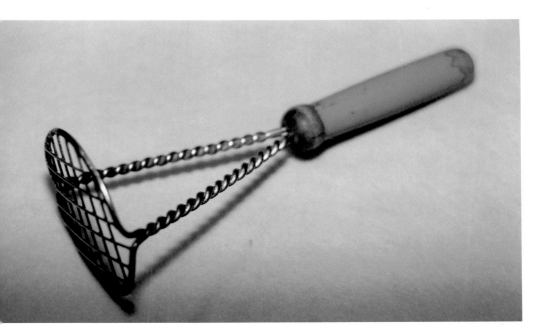

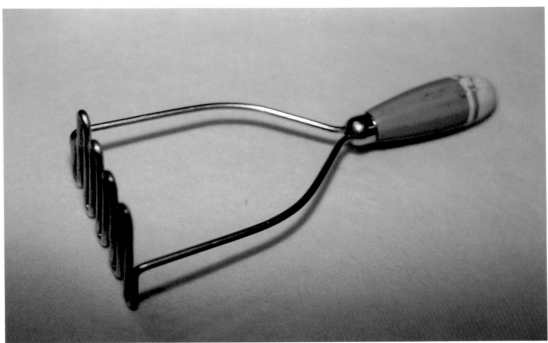

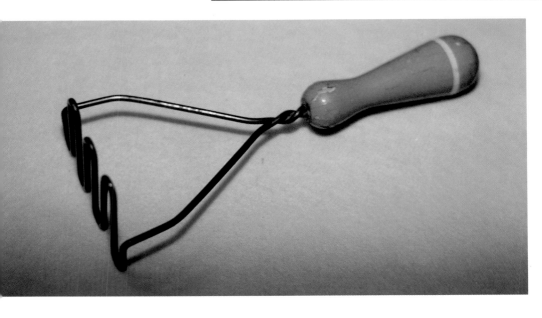

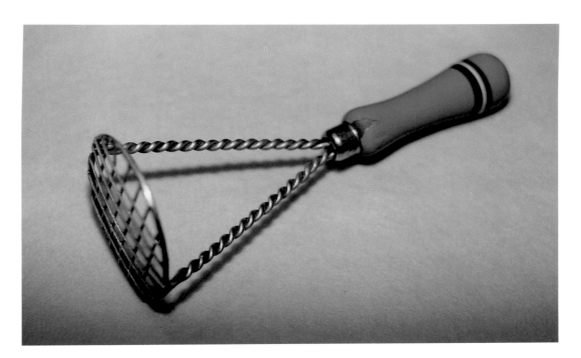

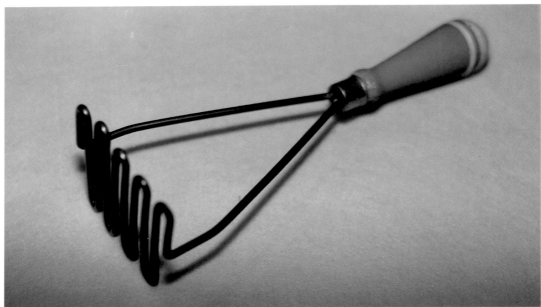

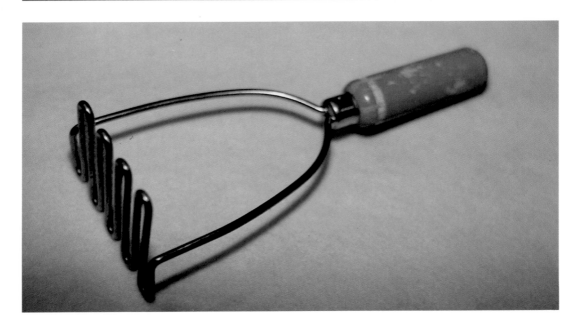

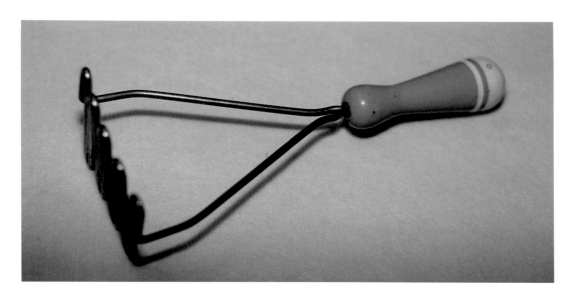

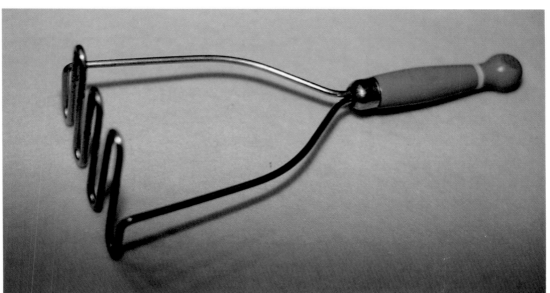

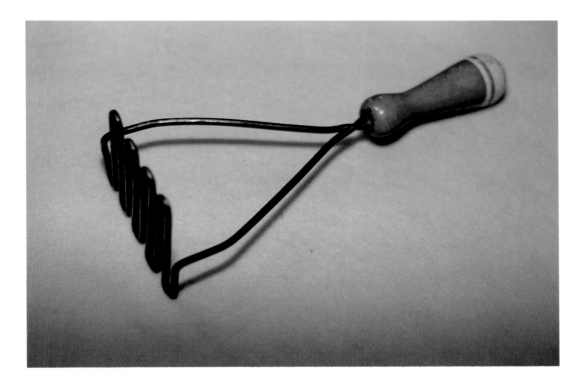

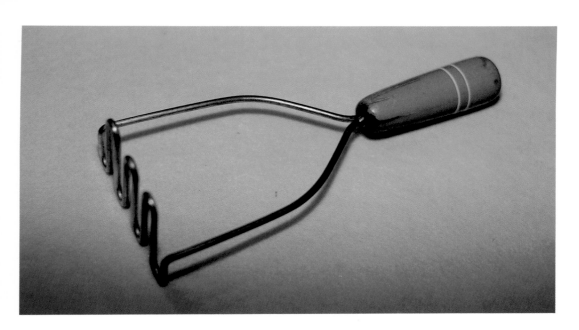

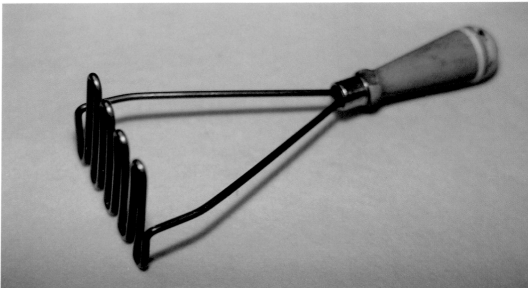

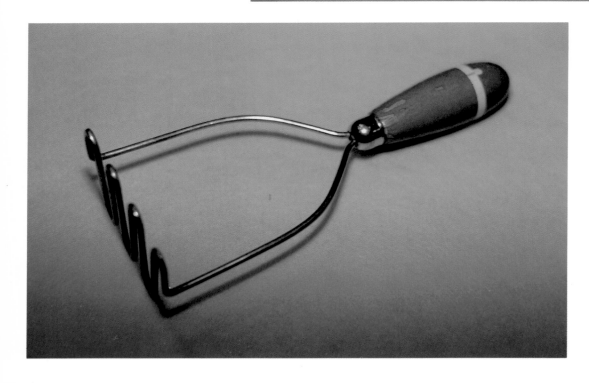

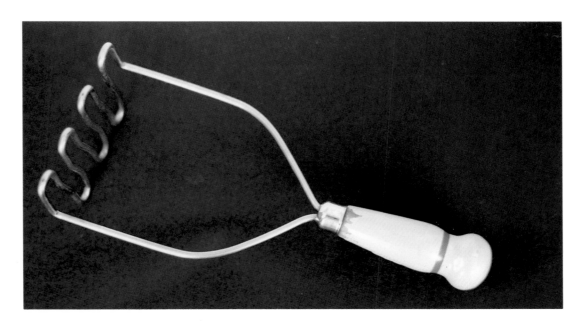

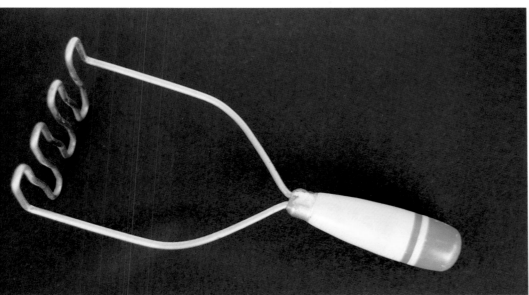

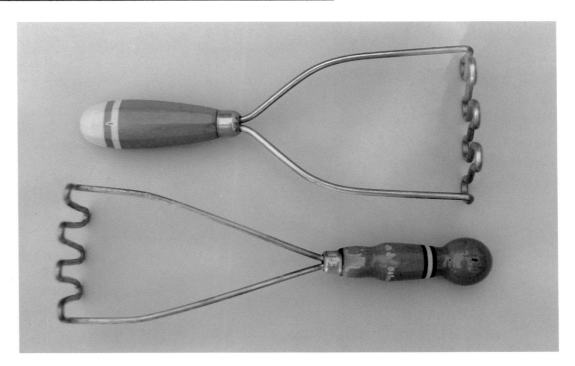

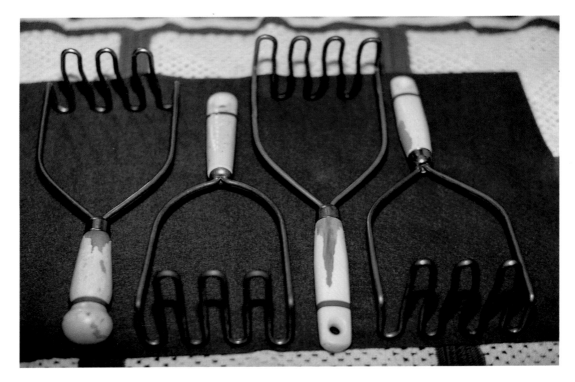

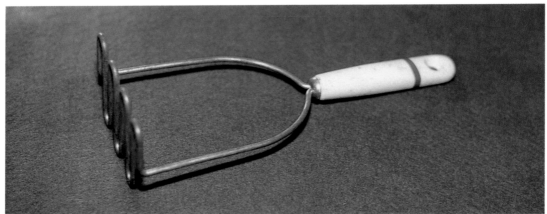

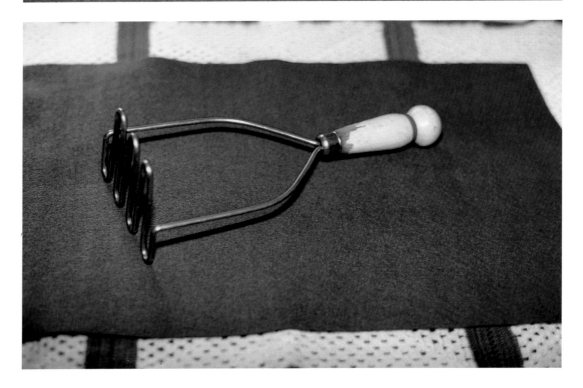

The following mashers should be found for about $15-22 each.

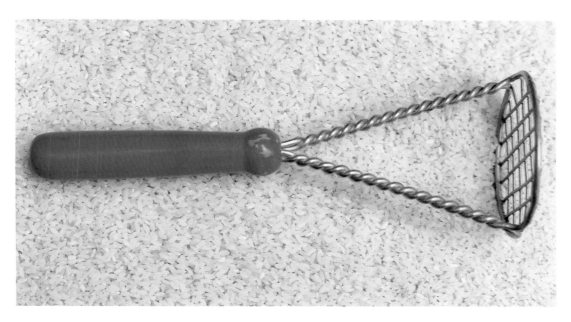

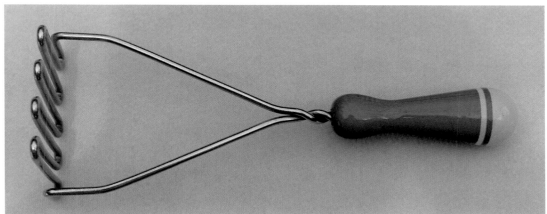

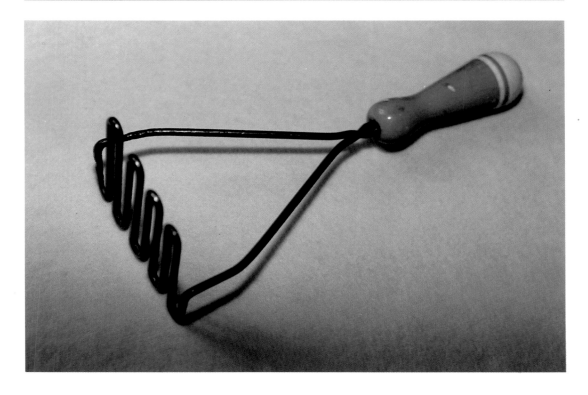

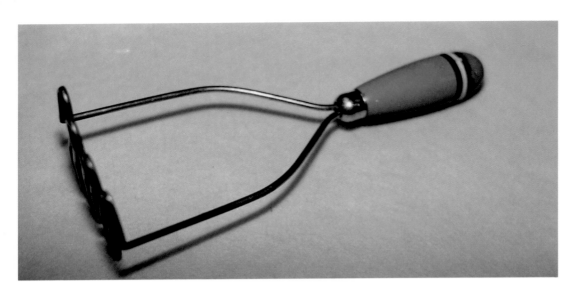

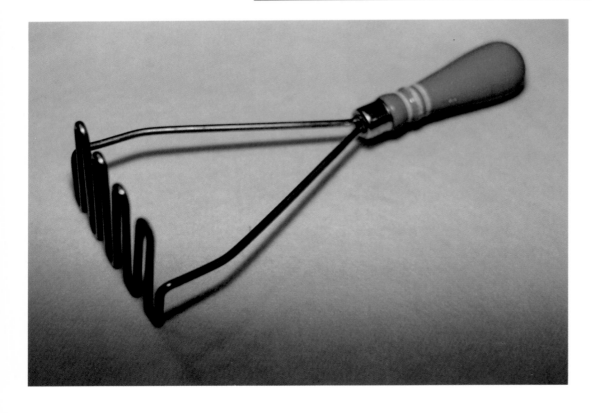

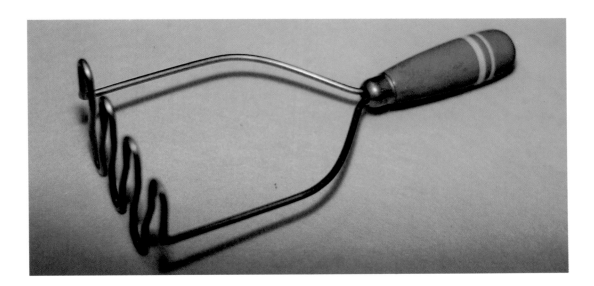

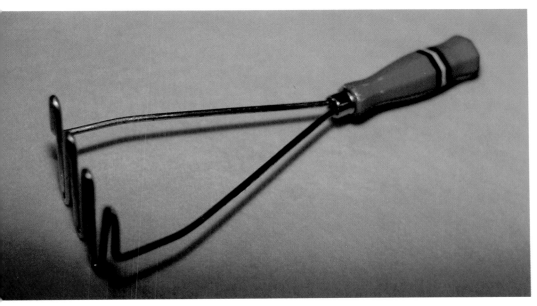

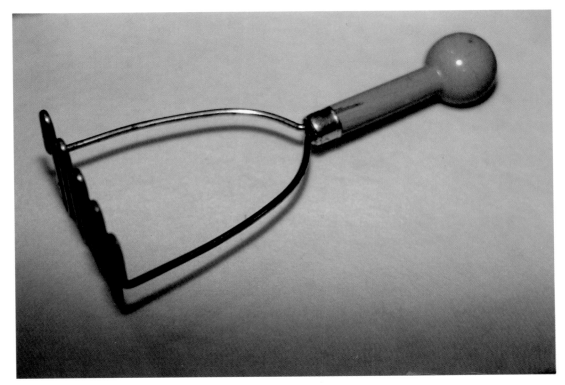

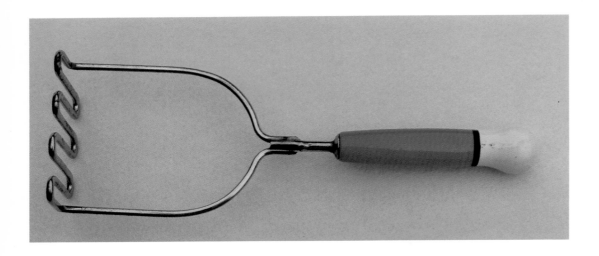

These hard-to-find potato mashers will cost between $25-35 each.

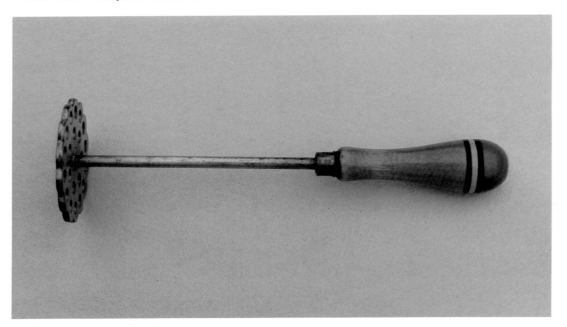

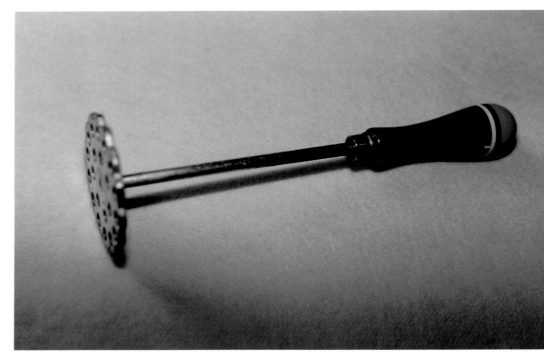

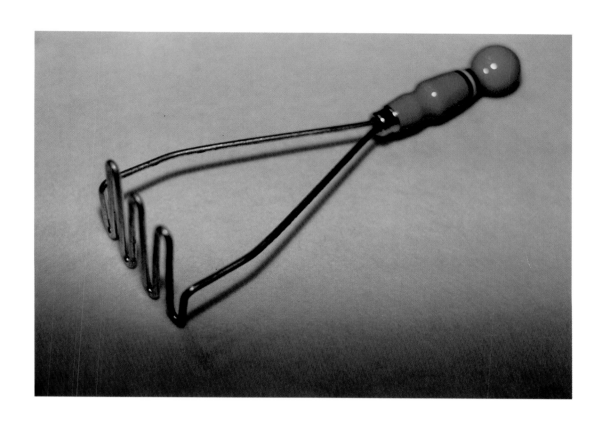

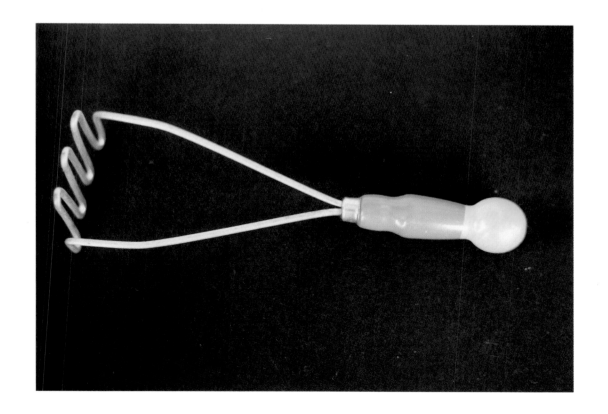

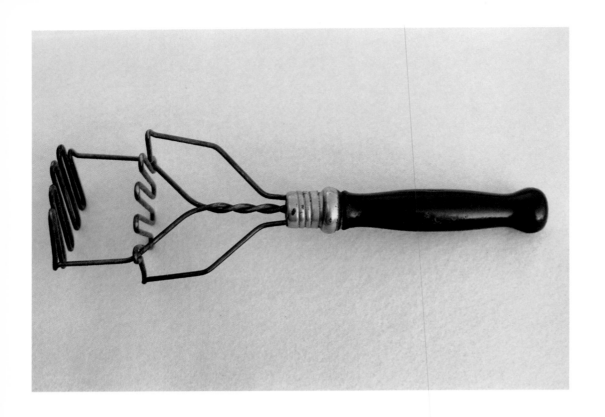

A&J's springloaded mechanical potato masher is worth $50-65 in working order with a handle in good condition as shown.

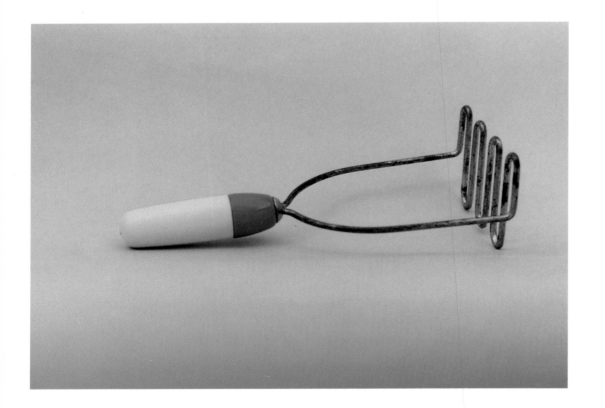

A plastic handled potato masher is not common. However due to the general lack of interest in this handle treatment its value remains at $12-15.

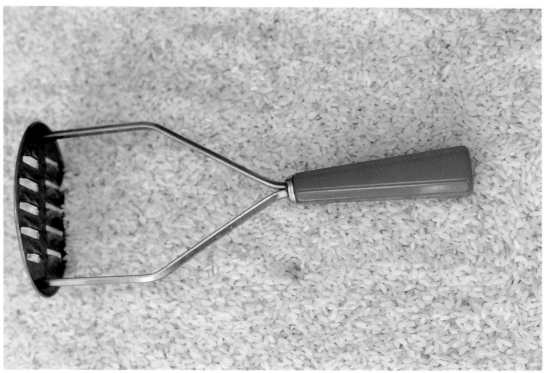

Bakelite handled potato mashers will cost from $30-35 apiece depending on the uniqueness of the handle design. $30-35

An impressive display of potato mashers circle this kitchen. Most are cleverly secured with a single nail, and the second picture shows this simply wonderful technique more clearly. As a point of interest, no two mashers are identical in this collection!

Green handled potato mashers mingle with old green mixing bowls on a wicker shelf. This charming display is in a living room, not a kitchen.

Recipe Boxes

Recipe boxes provide an organizational service still utilized today. Most are sized to accommodate standard 3 x 5" recipe cards and may be wood, metal, or plastic. Whether plain or decorative, most kitchens had at least one recipe box.

A winking chef greets the user of an all red unmarked metal recipe box. It holds 3 x 5" cards. $30-35.

Roosters decorate an all metal recipe box marked "The Beckhard Line Made in U.S.A." It holds standard 3 x 5" recipe cards. $30-35.

Ohio Art Company from Bryan, Ohio, made this metal recipe box to hold standard 3 x 5" cards. $20-25.

Cherries decorate the lid and front of this unusual recipe box that measures 7.25" high in the back, 6.25" high in the front, and 5.75" both across and deep. $35-40.

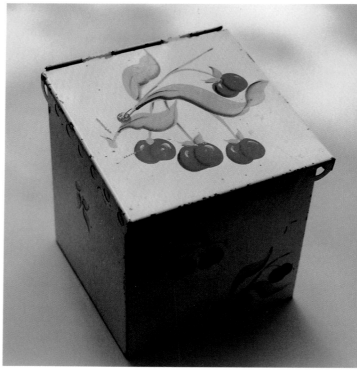

This wooden recipe box is marked "GOLD MEDAL FLOUR 'Kitchen-tested' RECIPES." Fourteen categories of recipes are included in the 5.75 x 4 x 3.5 inch oak box that originally cost $1.00. Coupons packed in Gold Medal Flour could be sent in for additional new recipes. $50-60

Precision Ware created this turquoise plastic recipe box with a chef's head on the front bottom piece to hold standard 3 x 5" cards. $40-45.

The 69 cent price is marked on the original sticker of a Lustro-ware Elegante recipe box. Even with rounded edges 3 x 5" cards fit inside. $30-35.

Refrigerator Dishes

Before the invention of Tupperware, how were leftovers stored? The answer is refrigerator dishes—round, square, and rectangular containers usually made of glass.

Refrigerator dishes are very collectible and can be quite costly. As items that received daily use, few have survived in chip-free condition. Glass aficionados must be willing to overlook nicks and chips from lids banging into bases. When a perfect piece is found, be prepared to pay more for its quality.

In this section you will find groupings of refrigerator dishes according to the manufacturer: "Crisscross" by Hazel Atlas, "Jennyware" by Jeannette Glass, "Ships" by McKee Glass, and a variety of others. The purpose of this presentation is to provide an overview, it is by no means a complete compilation of each company's pieces.

"Crisscross" was produced from 1936-1938. Today it is one of the most popular refrigerator set designs of all.

There are five different shapes in four colors—cobalt blue, crystal (clear), transparent green, and pink. The 5.5" refrigerator bowl with cover is not pictured. The three most familiar pieces are 4 x 4", 4 x 8", and 8 x 8". All have flat, handleless lids. The fifth piece is 3.5 x 5.75" and very closely resembles an inverted one pound butter dish.

Pricing is a reflection of supply and demand. Quite frankly, the supply of pink seems to be the least, followed by green. Crystal is the most abundant although not necessarily easy to find, and cobalt is slightly harder to find than crystal but much in demand. Expect to pay the least for crystal and the most for pink.

This refrigerator dish is often confused with a butter dish. Look in the butter dish section to see "Crisscross" one pound butters. The measurements are 3.5 x 5.25". Crystal $40, cobalt $175, green $100, pink $200.

This is the 4 x 8" refrigerator dish found in the same five combinations as the 4 x 4" dish. Crystal $20, crystal with cobalt $40, cobalt $140, green $75, pink $120.

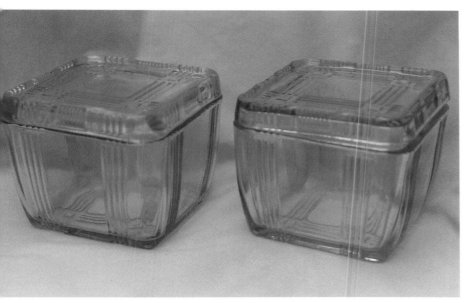

4 x 4" refrigerator dishes are available in all four colors plus a crystal base with a cobalt lid. crystal $15, crystal with cobalt lid $25, cobalt $45, green $40, pink $50.

Here are three sizes in transparent green. Not pictured is the 8 x 8" refrigerator dish, but the prices are provided. Crystal $30, crystal with cobalt $60, cobalt $160, green $95, pink $100.

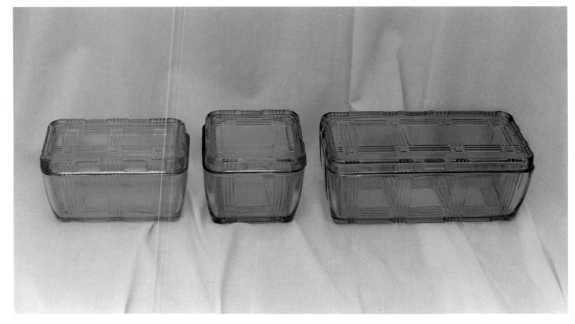

"Jennyware," like "Crisscross," was made from 1936-1938. Refrigerator dishes in this pattern are not easy to find.

The three colors used for "Jennyware" are crystal (clear), pink, and ultramarine (a teal-like blue-green). Refrigerator dishes are available in five sizes. The round ones are 16 ounces, 32 ounces, and 70 ounces, with handles recessed in such a way that they are flush with the lids. The other refrigerator dishes are 4.5 x 4.5" and 4.5 x 9" with no handles on these lids.

Finding "Jennyware" may be more difficult than affording it. Crystal will be the least expensive, followed by pink, and then ultramarine.

This picture shows the difference in lids. Square, $45; round, $70.

This ultramarine "Jennyware" refrigerator dish is 4.5 x 9". Crystal $25, pink $55, ultramarine $65.

"Ships" was made in red and black during the 1930s. I have no black examples included as they are virtually impossible to find in good condition. The pricing will be for red "Ships" only. Expect to pay more for black.

Refrigerator dishes were made in five sizes. The two four-sided pieces are 4 x 5" and 5 x 8" with clear handle-less lids. The three round refrigerator dishes are 10 ounces, 20 ounces, and 40 ounces. Round lids may be transparent or white and also have no handles.

Refrigerator dishes were often designed to "nest" together providing efficient use of refrigerator space. The first picture shows how three pieces fit together. The second arrangement allows a better view of the "Ships" pattern. 4 x 5" $35, 5 x 8" $55.

Here is a stack of all three round refrigerator dishes with white lids. A transparent lid is on the 40 ounce piece on the right. 10 ounces $35, 20 ounces $55, 40 ounces $75.

Delphite refrigerator pieces in perfect condition are very difficult to locate. Four different sizes and shapes are pictured. On the left, a rectangular refrigerator dish (which works nicely as a canister) is 4 x 4.75". The bottom center piece measures 4 x 8.25", and on it rests a refrigerator dish that is 4 x 4 inches. The round container on the right has a 32 ounce capacity. Although the pieces are unmarked they are from Jeannette Glass. Left (tall) $150, center (4 x 4.75") $70, center (4 x 8.25") $100, right (round) $185.

The design of these ultramarine refrigerator dishes may look familiar. These pieces are identical to the Jeannette Glass Company Delphite pieces in the previous picture. Ultramarine is as elusive as Delphite. Left (square) $40, right (rectangle) $65.

Of all the colors presented Chalaine is the most difficult to find. Pictured are the 24 and 48 ounce round refrigerator dishes. Other sizes and shapes were made in Chalaine but are rare indeed! Left (large) $100, right (small) $120.

The first Pyrex refrigerator dishes included a 1.5 quart yellow, 1.5 pint blue, and two 1.5 cup red containers. They were marketed as oven, refrigerator, and freezer sets because of their tolerance of extreme temperatures. Set of four $50-75.

A set of four Pyrex refrigerator dishes was $3.45 according to an April 1956 edition of *Ladies' Home Journal*.

Refrigerator sets were made by Corning Glass in a variety of solid colors and patterns as shown in these two pictures. Expect to pay $10-20 apiece for any of these 1.5 cup refrigerator dishes.

Lids for Pyrex refrigerator sets were originally produced with two groupings of narrow ridges as shown on the right. Consumers found these difficult to keep clean so after 1950 Corning Glass Works changed the design to larger ridges as shown on the left.

McKee Glass Company produced a three piece refrigerator set with two 4 x 5" dishes and one 5 x 8" dish. Fired-on glass is just becoming very popular again. $60-75 set of three, $20 each.

Pieces were sometimes produced to promote a business. These French casseroles/refrigerator dishes are labeled: "Net Content 12 oz. Pensupreme Creamed Cottage Cheese Dist. By Penn Dairies, Inc." Purchase of this cottage cheese gave the consumer a 7" long, 2" deep reusable piece of Glasbake. $15 each with lid, $8 without lid.

Sunburst patented these aluminum 4.5 x 5.25 x 1.75" refrigerator dishes. A growing interest in aluminum kitchen pieces makes these very collectible. $12-15 each.

Ricers

Ricers were normally used for making mashed potatoes or apple sauce. There are variations in the number and placement of holes in the food receptacle, but otherwise they are relatively standard.

If purchasing a ricer for use examine it carefully for rust.

Handy Thing Mfg. Co., Ludington, Michigan, produced the Handy Potato Ricer/Fruit Press. It originally sold for $2.59. A white handle is not commonly found. $15-18.

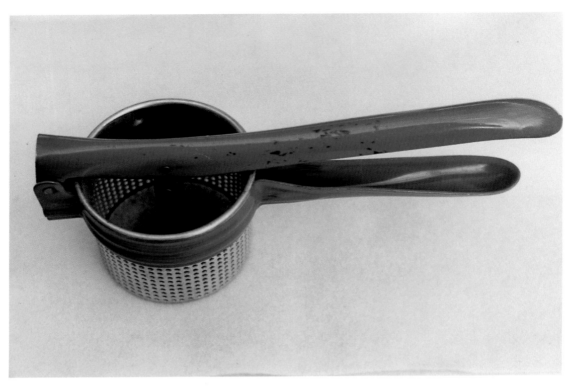

Red handled ricers are the easiest to locate. $12-15.

The holes in this green handled ricer are only at the bottom of the
food receptacle. Green is a difficult handle color to find. $12-15.

Rolling Pins

Rolling pins are easily recognized by most everyone, and are often still actively used in even the most modernly equipped kitchens. When it's time to roll out dough there just isn't more effective technology than a rolling pin.

Most rolling pins are all wood. Aluminum, chrome, and glass rolling pins were also produced, but only wood and aluminum rolling pins are pictured here.

Since rolling pins are still being produced, here is a way to help select an older one rather than a newer one. Look carefully where the handles meet the center rolling piece. There should not be a plastic ring where these come together if the rolling pin is older.

Red handled rolling pins will cost from $12-18 each.

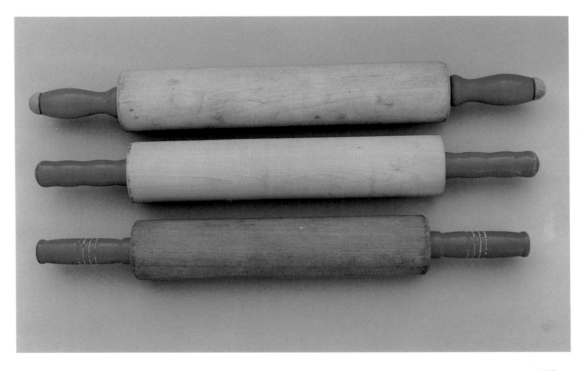

Blue handled rolling pins are uncommon. $25-30.

The dark blue rolling pin shown on top is much more difficult to find than the green ones in this and the following picture. Blue $20-25, green $15-20 each.

This yellow handled rolling pin retains original paint in excellent condition. $10-15.

Shiny black handles look almost new on this rolling pin. $20-25.

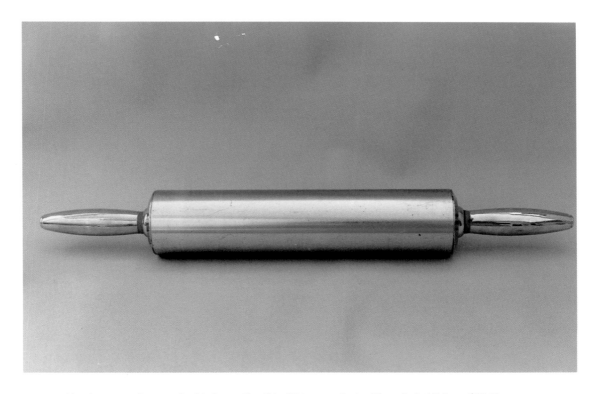

Aluminumware is a popular kitchen collectible. This unmarked rolling pin is 18" long. $20-25.

Sandwich Makers

Sandwich makers were designed for toasting sandwiches over gas and wood-burning stoves or any other open flame. Today they can add a pleasant, nostalgic look by a fireplace. Sandwich makers provide a touch of the past and since they can also still be used, a taste of the past.

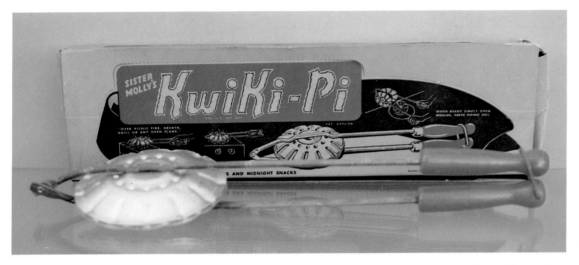

"Sister Molly's Kwiki-Pi" was made by Morris Mfg. Co. Asbury Park and Belmar, New Jersey. It is 15" long with red wooden handles. $20-25 with box, $15-20 without box.

The twin silver stripes on the blue handles indicates a Nutbrown product. Made in England, the "Sandwich Toaster" is 14" long. $25-28.

A "Snack-Toaster" by Federal Mfg. & Eng. Corp. is unusual because of its double feature allowing for two sandwiches to be prepared simultaneously. $25-30.

Scoops

Wooden handled scoops were measurement devices when cooking or baking, a size increment being indicated on the metal. Because they were particularly helpful items they received much use and wear. Finding scoops, especially the half-cup size, can be difficult. Locating scoops whose wooden handles retained their original paint may be challenging.

The focus of this section is on these quarter-cup and half-cup scoops. Only a small sample of other kinds of scoops is provided.

At 7.5" in length, an A&J green handled scoop is marked "Level full ¼ cup." $15-20.

"Level full ½ cup" identifies a 9.5" long green handled A&J scoop, a hard size to find. $15-20.

The difference between this A&J half-cup scoop and the previous one is the handle treatment. $15-20.

EKCO A&J made this "Level full ¼ cup" scoop in yellow with one green stripe. $15-20.

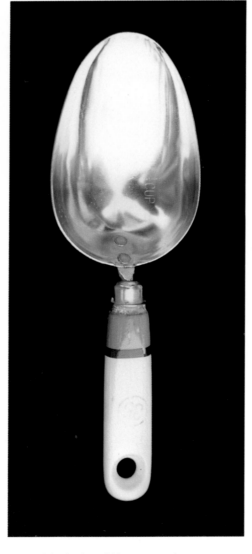

The original price of 35 cents remains on an Androck "Level full ¼ cup" scoop. $15-20.

A rarely found A&J "Level full ½ cup" scoop is in red and white. $15-20.

"Level full ¼ cup" marks this EKCO scoop with a less popular handle. $12-15.

A stubby red and white handle is used for an Androck "Level full ¼ cup" scoop that measures 6.5" in length. $15-20.

White with blue is a less common handle coloration. A&J's "Level full ¼ cup" scoop is 7.25" long. $15-20.

Two A&J scoops are marked "Level full ¼ cup." $15-20 each.

EKCO A&J manufactured this "Level full ¼ cup" scoop. $15-20.

This ¼ cup A&J scoop is 7.5" long. $15-20.

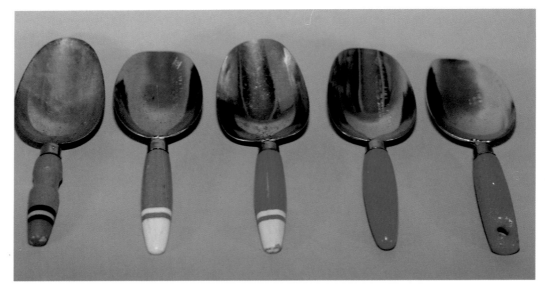

Five handle treatments of ¼ cup scoops are shown. $15-20 each.

Red and white plastic is used for a handle on Androck's "Level full ¼ cup" scoop that is 7.75" long. $12-15.

The yellow plastic scoop advertises a hatchery in Cochranville, Pennsylvania, and is 8" long. The aluminum scoop, only 5.25" in length, is marked Germany. plastic $12-15, aluminum $3-5.

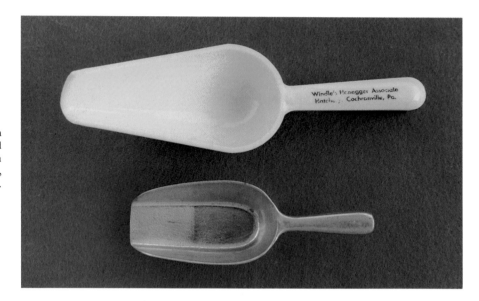

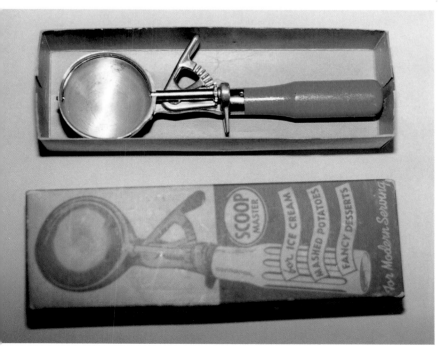

Bonny Products Co. from New York marketed the Scoop Master "for ice cream, mashed potatoes, (and) fancy desserts." It is wooden handled, 8.5" long, and unmarked. $25-30 without box, $35-40 with box.

The Peerless ice cream scoop is almost 8.5" long with a plastic handle. $15-20.

Depressing the yellow lever pushes a dip of ice cream from Lloyd Disher Company's 7.75" plastic ice cream scoop. $10-15.

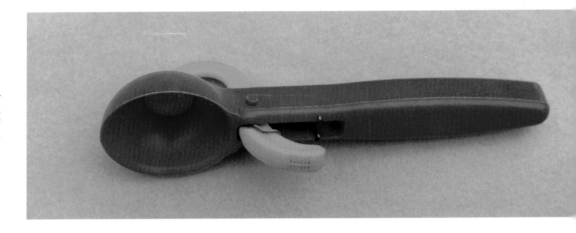

SHORT'NING AND ICE CREAM SPOON

This copper colored "SHORT 'NING AND ICE CREAM SPOON" measures 7.75" in length. $12-15.

Shakers

Milk glass flour, sugar, salt, pepper, and spice shakers come in a colorful assortment of designs. They are normally short, about 3"; or tall, about 8". Some may have "Roman Arches" a series of three curved shoulders going up two sides but not the front or back.

A number of the lids in these photographs have been repainted, and not necessarily in their original colors. All of the shakers in this section are from one collection. It has been a loving task searching for years to assemble such an impressive display, often purchasing shakers one at a time.

When buying, look for pieces with bright shiny colors. Lids can be repainted or replaced so the important factor is the integrity of the glass. The shakers speak for themselves so only prices are provided. Items with faded colors would be of lesser value.

Red sailboats (pair) $75
Green sailboats (pair) $65
Red & blue sailboats (pair) $50

"Ships" $40 each

Red tulips $40 each

Tulips (pair) $75
Checkered flowers (pair) $120

Tall cattails (pair) $80
Short cattails (pair) $50

Windmills (pair) $25
Dutch figures $18 each

Hats (pair) $65
Swans (pair) $80

Hand painted fruit (pair)
$30
Apples (pair) $75

Dutch figures (pair, either
size) $65

Windmills (pair) $45
Dutch figures (pair) $65

Birds on circles (pair) $80

Birds on branch (pair) $120
Butter dish or grease jar $300

Dutch figures (pair) $120
Mexican (single) $45
Flowers (pair) $75

Small woman with churn
(pair) $65
Tall woman with churn
(pair) $85

Flowers $45 each

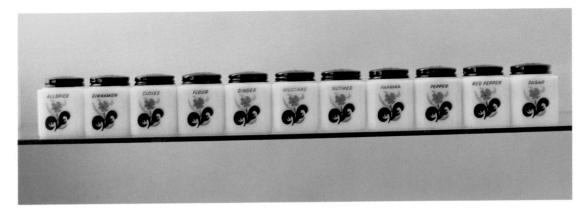

Flowers $30 each

Small red flowers $50 each

Short shakers with red flowers $40 each Tall shakers $50 each

Cinnamon $50
Niagara Falls (pair) $65
Rings (pair) $85
Girl in garden (pair) $85

Gate $60 each

Poinsettias $40 each

Three red flowers $40 each

Basket of flowers (tall) $50 pair
Basket of flowers (short) $40 pair

Basket of flowers (small individual spices) $20 each
Basket of flowers (flour or sugar) $20 each

Red and green flowers $40 each

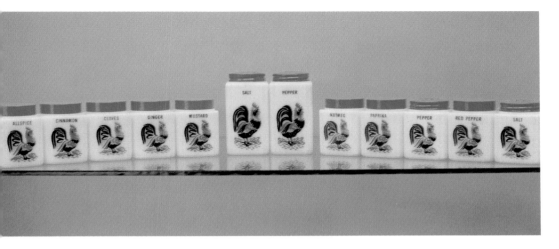

Roosters $30 each

Yellow and red flowers $30 each

Yellow flowers $40 each

Cherries $30 each

THE HERB CHEST (top row) $20 each The Spice Chest (bottom row) $20 each

Girl watering flowers (yellow paint not original) $50 each

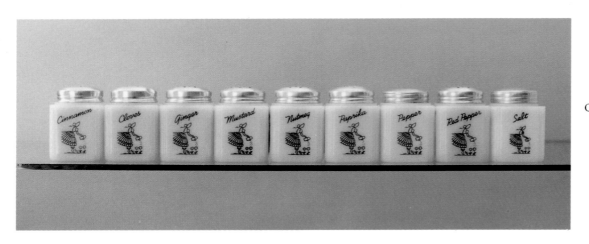

Girl watering flowers $50 each

Scotties (tall) $65 each
Scotties (short) $65 each
Scotties butter dish or grease jar $300

Blue figures $18 each

Some shaker lids had no holes for pouring. Here are different hole arrangements on the lids that do.

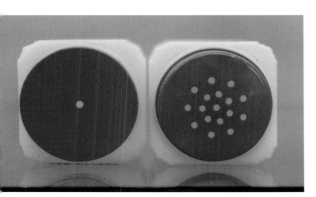

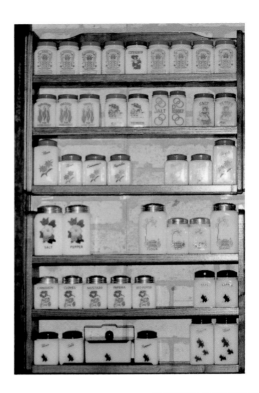

Here is a partial view of the collection presented. Shelves of
shakers surround this kitchen in a colorful display.

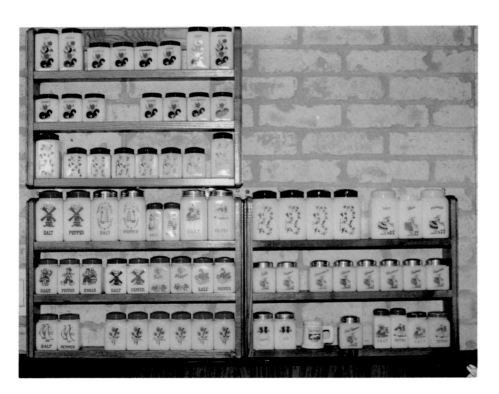

Sharpeners

There are two basic knife sharpening designs. The first is to draw a knife blade through sharpening disks. The second is to rub a blade against a sharpening surface.

Wooden handles are most common, however bakelite was used when the sharpener was part of a three-piece carving set. Included here are a china handle and an all-metal sharpener as well.

Of the vast array of gadgets, knife sharpeners are the least recognized item from the past. Many collectors merely select a sharpener because the handle treatment matches other items in a collection. Look for original paint in good condition and minimal deterioration of the metal parts.

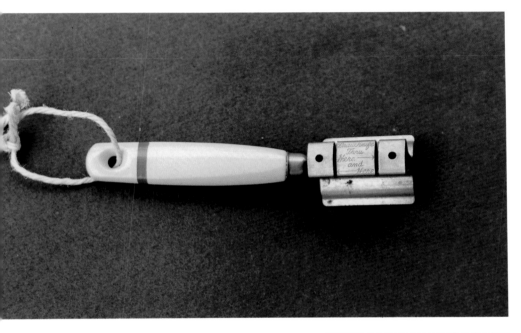

"Draw Knife Thru Here and Here" instructs the user of EKCO A&J's 6.75" knife sharpener. $12-15.

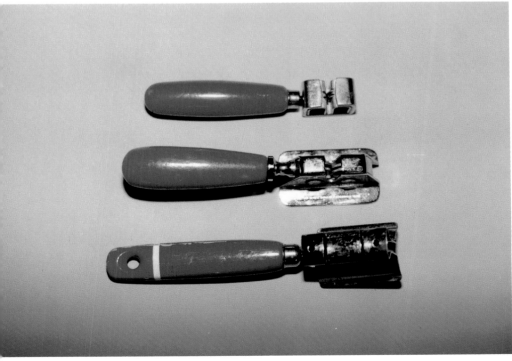

Three manufacturers produced similar yet different red wooden handled sharpeners. On top is "ROTARY" which at 5.25" is from England. Also English is the 6.25" "Challenge." The bottom knife sharpener is from A&J and measures 7" in length. $10-12 each.

EKCO's bakelite handled sharpener is 7" long. $8-10.

A bottle opener is on the end of an unmarked 7" long knife sharpener. $8-10.

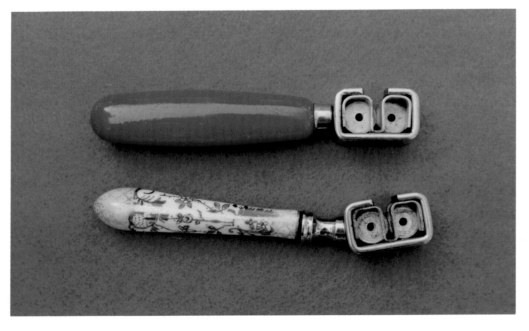

The top sharpener is shown earlier in this section. However this shows a different view and pairs it with another piece also from A.E. Louis & Co. in England. The bottom knife sharpener has a china handle and is marked Loraine. Top $10-12, bottom $15-18.

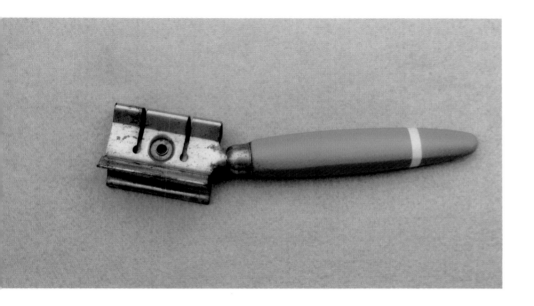

A green handled 6.5" long sharpener is marked "Draw Knife Thru Here and Here." $15-18.

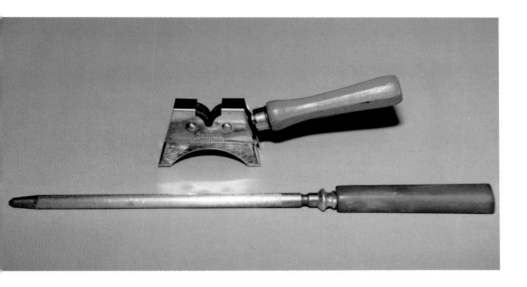

Both knife sharpeners have green handles but the similarities end here. The wooden handled sharpener from Eversharp in Bridgeport, Connecticut, is 6.5" long. The 12.5" long unmarked sharpening steel has a bakelite handle and is part of a carving set. Wood $12-15, bakelite $20-25.

The "KANTBREAK" sharpener from Norton Abrasives is 15" long and has an unusual blue handle. $15-20.

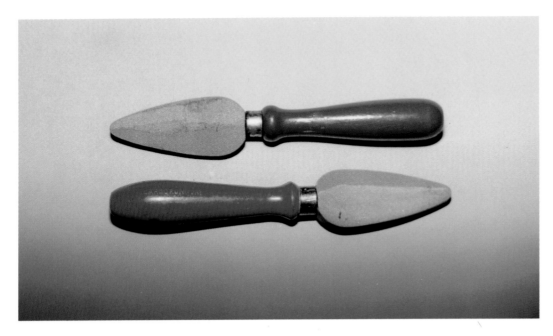

Carborundum Trade Mark is on the red handled sharpener, the green handled one is unmarked. Both are 7.5" long. $12-15 each.

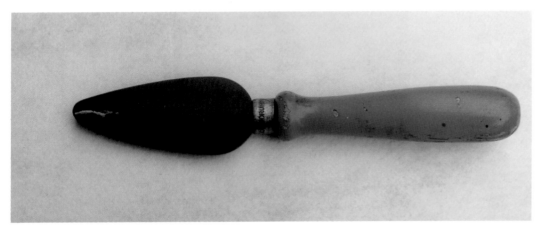

A Carborundum sharpener is 7.25" long with a blue wooden handle. $12-15.

This 5 Star Handy Tool is a wonderful example of ingenuity. For $2.50 the 6.5" long gadget is a knife sharpener, glass cutter, scissors, sharpener, bottle opener, and lawn mower sharpener. $8-10 with box, $5-7 without box.

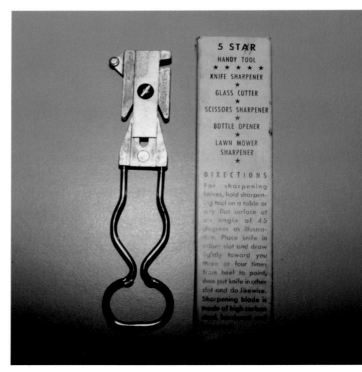

Sifters

The colors and styles of sifters vary tremendously. They may be plain or accessory pieces that match canisters, bread boxes, and other kitchen metalware. Some operate by turning a knob on top, others have a crank to rotate, and many have a squeeze lever at the handle.

Early sifters were plain tin. Later they were produced with simple coloration, a stripe of color or a solid color with a stripe or two for accent. As kitchen tools changed from being purely functional to decorated pieces, the sifter also evolved.

This section provides a sample of sifter designs from the very plain to highly decorative. All are in working order, so they can still do the job for which they were produced.

Many sifters are triple screened like this Bromwell Aerator. It is marked "THREE PADDLE AGITATORS MAKE THE FLOUR FLUFFY FOR AERATED CAKE AND BREAD." Two views show the front and large red handle on the back. $20-25.

The tin sifter on the left has a red plastic handle and no markings. Nesco's "VIS-IBLE MEASURE FLOUR SIFTER SIFTS, AERATES, FLUFFS" and has a red, wooden knob handle. Left $7-10, right $8-12.

Androck's two cup sifter has two black wooden handles. $10-15.

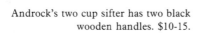

This Androck three screen-four cup one hand sifter originally sold for $1.69. $12-15.

One cup sifters are hard to find and in high demand by collectors. A black wooden knob is on this Rusridge one cup sifter. $15-20.

No manufacturer is shown on this one cup sifter with a green knob handle. $20-25.

Colors of the early 1930s are reflected on this triple screen sifter. No manufacturer is marked on this piece. $20-25.

The design of this sifter is repeated in green in the next picture. Other metal kitchen items were made with this motif. $15-20.

Two different sifters share the popular apple design. Bromwell's three cup sifter sold for 45 cents and has a white background. H.L. Green sold this unmarked sifter with a buff background for 39 cents. $40-45 each as shown with original prices, $30-35 each unpriced.

Androck produced the three screen sifter on the right. The sifter on the left, as its mate in the previous picture, is unmarked. $15-20 each.

Use of color is the only difference between these "three screens" sifters. $15-20 each.

Tomatoes decorate an unmarked sifter. $35-40.

No markings are shown on these two sifters that appear to be from one manufacturer. They have the same series of ridges in the metal, the same metal handle, and the same red wooden knob. $15-20 left, $30-35 right.

A wheat motif decorates two Androck Hand-I-Sifts that differ only in handle color. $30-35 each.

One of the most popular sifters of all is this Androck Hand-I- Sift three screen sifter. $65-70 if mint, $45-50 as shown with some wear.

Slicers

Cheese, egg, and tomato slicers are pictured in this section. They are simple tools designed for one task.

Cheese slicers are of two styles. The first utilizes a wire and the second a thin piece of metal for cutting.

Egg slicers have a row of wires for multiple, simultaneous cuts.

Tomato slicers use a row of serrated cutting edges for slicing numerous, thin, even pieces.

If purchasing a cutter for use be sure to carefully examine all cutting surfaces and choose an item in rust-free condition. Cheese slicers are plentiful and in low demand so they will not be expensive. Egg slicers are not costly either, and are readily purchased if in an unusual color. Red wooden handled tomato slicers are also abundant. Finding handles with colors other than red may be a challenge.

This cheese slicer came in many different colored bakelite handles. It is very common. $25-30.

Household Specialties in Union, New Jersey, made a wooden handled cheese slicer which is "ideal for cutting ice cream, butter, bananas, and eggs." $20-25 with original package, $10-15 without original package.

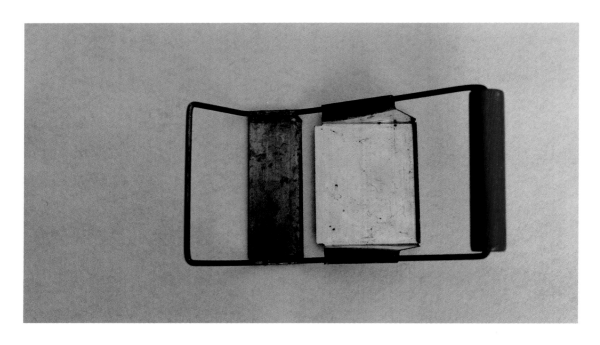

"Detroit U.S.A. Pat. Pending" marks an 8" long cheese slicer. $15-20.

An unusual blue handle is on this unmarked cheese slicer. $12-15.

MEDCO from New York City patented these two egg slicers. $12-15 each.

This tomato slicer is 10.75" long. The yellow and green handle is very hard to find. $10-15.

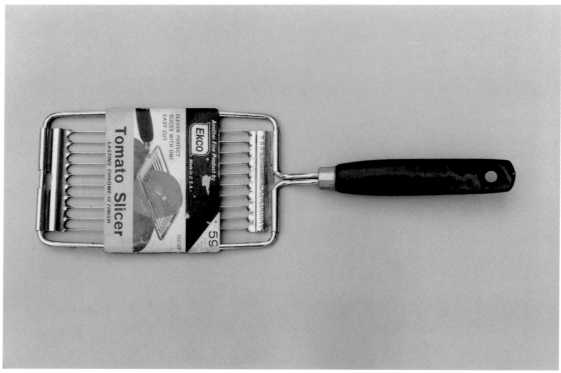

Fifty-nine cents would buy any of the three tomato slicers from EKCO. They are all 11.25" long. $7-10 without sleeves, $10-15 with original sleeves.

Spatulas

The sizes, shapes, and designs of spatulas are never ending. The following selection of sixteen wood and plastic handled spatulas is only the beginning of all the possibilities.

Spatulas were heavily used in many kitchens and this is evident on the majority of surviving pieces. On some, the handles may have retained their original paint but the metal is scratched, pitted, or rusted. On others the handles may be worn down to bare wood. The search for a near-perfect spatula with a specific handle treatment may be a challenge but not an impossibility.

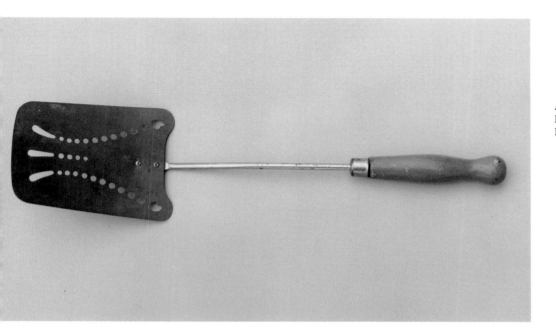

An unmarked 12.75" long green handled spatula has an unusual hole pattern. $12-15.

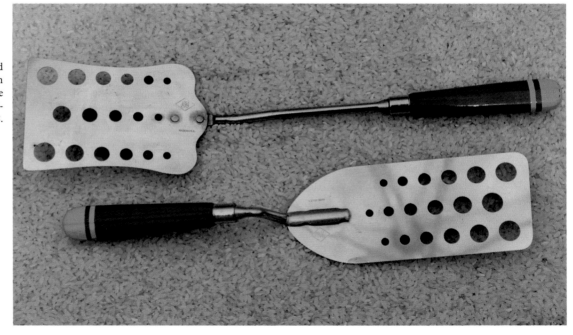

Two A&J spatulas are marked "Chromium Plated" on their green wooden handles. The bottom one is in exceptional condition. Top $8-10, bottom $15-18.

Here are two more A&J spatulas. The green one on the top is 13.75" long with a less common handle treatment. The yellow and green spatula on the bottom is 12.25" long. Top $15-18, bottom $10-12.

Although yellow handles are not as popular as other colors, this A&J spatula is in excellent condition and in the difficult-to-find 8.5" length. $12-15.

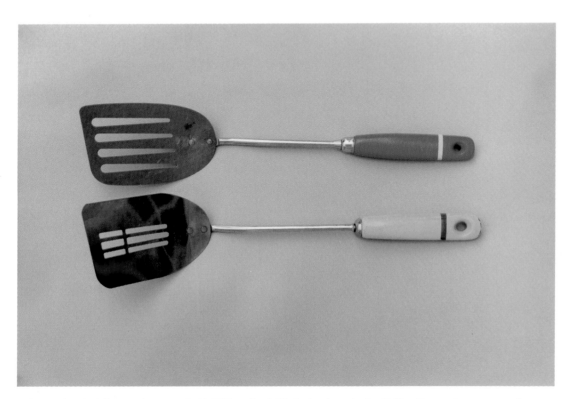

The red and white spatula on top is 13.75" long by A&J. Androck made the 13.5" yellow and green example on the bottom. $12-15 each.

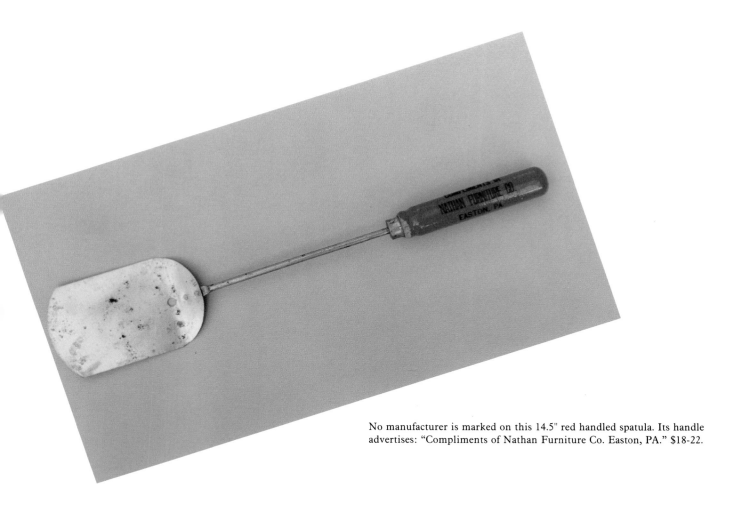

No manufacturer is marked on this 14.5" red handled spatula. Its handle advertises: "Compliments of Nathan Furniture Co. Easton, PA." $18-22.

A blue-green handle is on this spatula with diamond-shaped holes. It is 13" long and unmarked. Although this is a unique spatula its lack of companion pieces suppresses its value. $12-15.

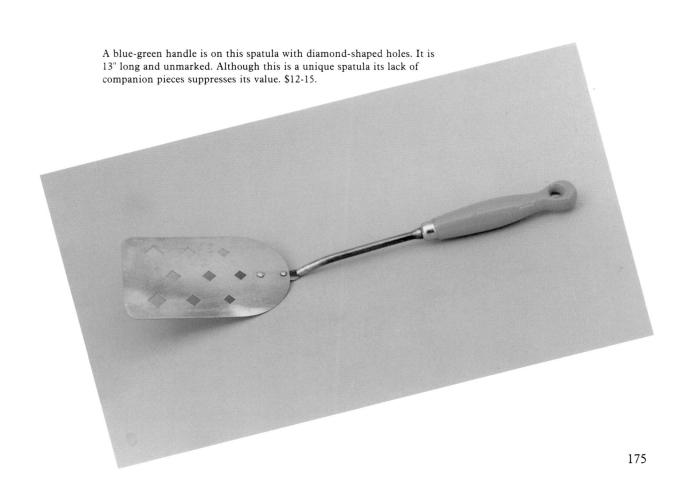

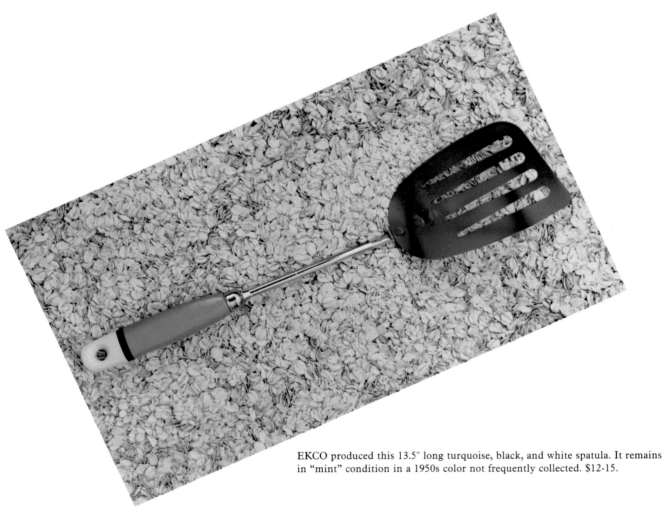

EKCO produced this 13.5" long turquoise, black, and white spatula. It remains in "mint" condition in a 1950s color not frequently collected. $12-15.

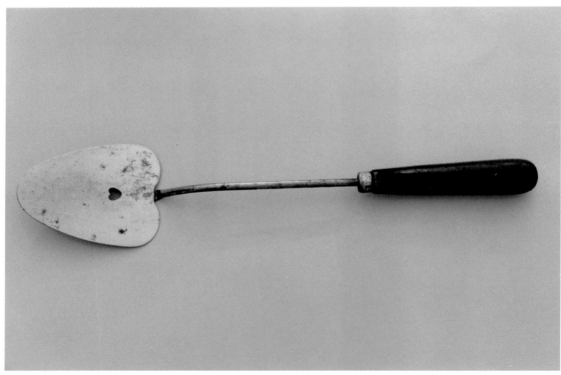

A heart-shaped hole is echoed in this heart-shaped spatula with a black wooden handle. Unmarked, it is 12.5" long with unfortunate deterioration on the metal. $10-12 as shown, $18-20 if mint.

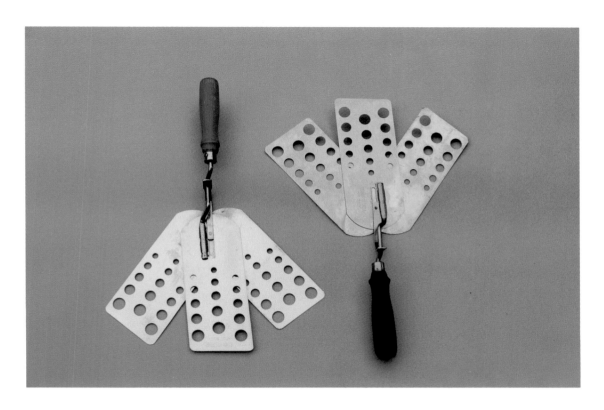

These spatulas open and close with the push of a lever near the red or black handle. Both are 10.75" long and marked "Stainless Steel Made in U.S.A." $15-20.

Here are two spatulas with plastic handles. Androck made the 13.5" red and white example on top. The 9.25" turquoise spatula on the bottom was produced by EKCO. $8-10 each.

Spoons

It's hard to find a more basic kitchen item than a spoon. Whether for stirring or serving, a spoon is a piece of standard equipment. Wooden, bakelite, and plastic handled spoons range from lengths of about 10.25" to 12.25", so no further length descriptions will be provided.

The differences between spoons worth noting are the handle treatments and clever variations, such as the measuring spoon and scraping spoon.

As with any well-used kitchen tool, the collector's challenge is finding an item in near mint condition, and the ultimate reward is accumulating a variety of spoons with the same handle treatment.

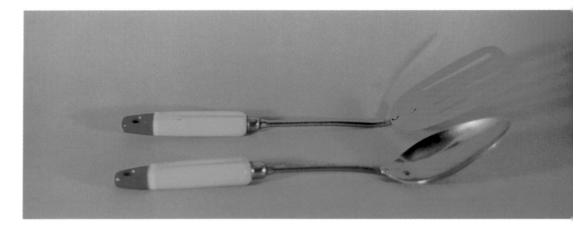

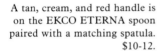

A tan, cream, and red handle is on the EKCO ETERNA spoon paired with a matching spatula. $10-12.

On top is a slotted vegetable spoon by EKCO A&J. Below is an A&J spoon in superior condition. Top as shown $5-8, top if mint $10-12, bottom $10-15.

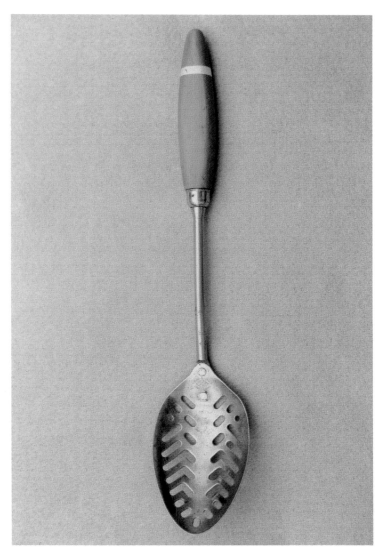

Androck also produced a spoon with the yellow and green handle. As shown $5-8, if mint $10-12.

This 12.75" long green handled straining spoon was made by A&J. $12-18.

These A&J spoons are in superior condition. $15-20 each.

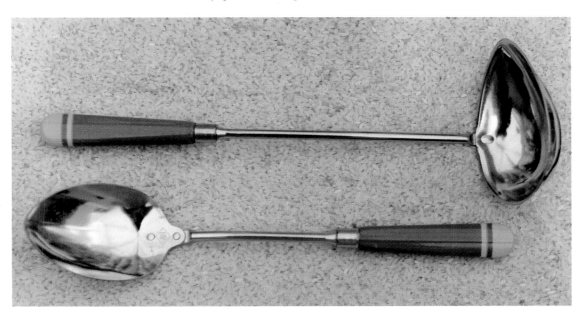

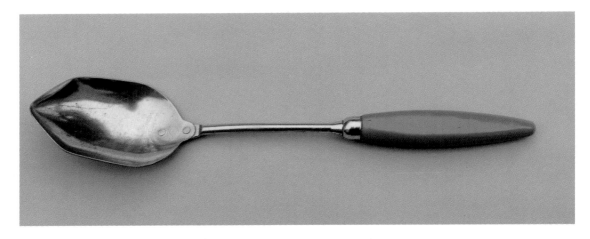

A&J patented this green handled spoon marked, "Scraper spoon gets the corners." $15-20.

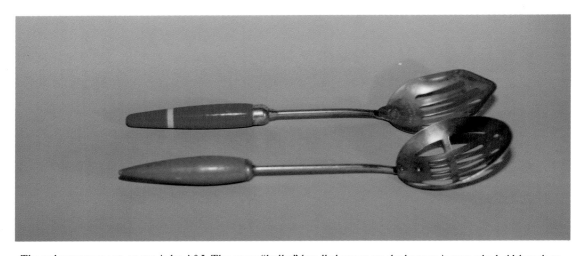

The red scraper spoon on top is by A&J. The green "bullet" handled spoon on the bottom is unmarked. Although an uncommon handle, the "bullet" on cooking utensils is not frequently sought by collectors. Red $15-20, green $15-20.

The tri-colored spoon on top is an unusual handle treatment from Androck. EKCO made the spoon on the bottom. Both have chrome shafts. $10-15 each.

The worn condition of these spoons reduces their value. However, all have less common handles. Another example of the top spoon is shown in the next picture with improved but not perfect metal. $7-10 each as shown.

The 11.25" bakelite measuring spoon on top includes the following gradations: "Full 2 TABLESPOONS, 1 TABLESPOON, 2 TEASPOONS, 1 TEASPOON." A&J made the 12.25" long red wooden handled spoon on the bottom. Top (bakelite) $25-30, bottom (wood) $10-15.

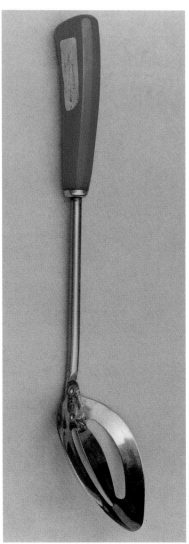

This 12.5" long red bakelite handled spoon retains a barely legible sticker advertising a business in Pennsylvania. It is "Corona Quality Stainless Steel." $25-30.

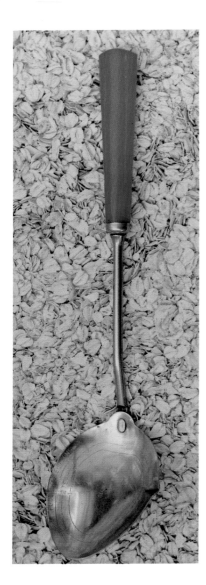

The stainless steel bowl of this bakelite spoon has measurements for one and two teaspoons and one and two tablespoons. A pour spout allows ease in use. $25-30

Plastic handled kitchen gadgets are not as popular as wood and bakelite handles. This will influence the price of these stainless steel EKCOLINE spoons. $12-15 each.

EKCOLINE Win Grip Kitchen Tools are advertised in an April 1948 issue of *Ladies' Home Journal*. They picture nine different gadgets with red and white plastic handles.

Ray J. Walther Company from Des Moines, Ohio, produced the "Tallstirs" aluminum iced tea spoons here in their original box. $20-25 as packaged, $15-18 set of six without package.

Spreaders

The nomenclature for this next grouping of kitchenware includes spreaders, servers, spatulas, and paddles. In this book they will be referred to as spreaders, often utilized for spreading icing. Two photographs pair a spreader with a pastry server, recognizable by its broader metal surface.

Spreaders were produced in the handle treatments seen on other gadgets. Although they are not found in abundance, when located they tend to be in relatively unworn condition.

Overall dimensions are fairly standard at about 11.5" in length. Most are unmarked.

Examples are provided with wood and bakelite handles. Select wooden handled spreaders with original paint in good condition. Bakelite handles should be examined for cracks. Perhaps because the metal was not stainless steel, spreader blades can be "pitted." Consider the overall condition when making a purchase.

At 10.5" in length this is the shortest spreader presented. Yellow with a red stripe is an uncommon handle treatment. $15-20.

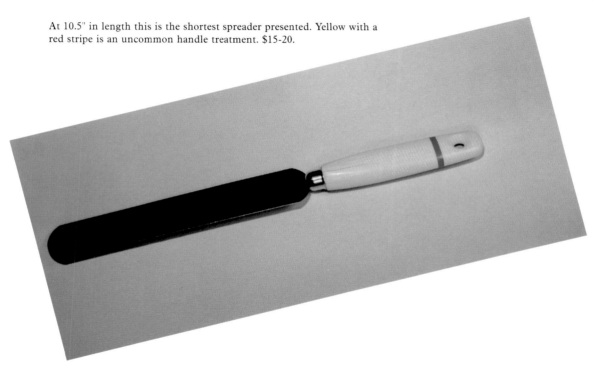

Typically this 11.5" spreader is unmarked. $10-15.

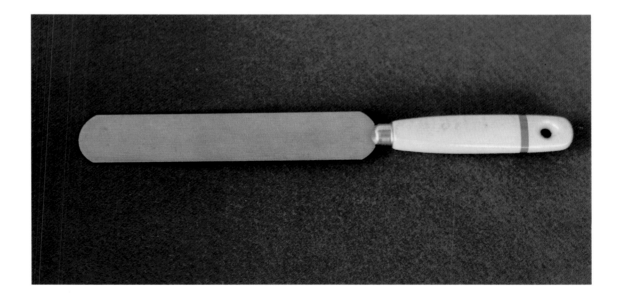

EKCO A&J made the fork and spatula. The spreader appears to match but is unmarked. $10-15.

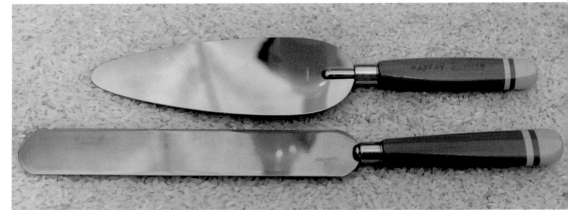

A&J made the 11.25" long spreader shown with a matching pastry server. $15-20.

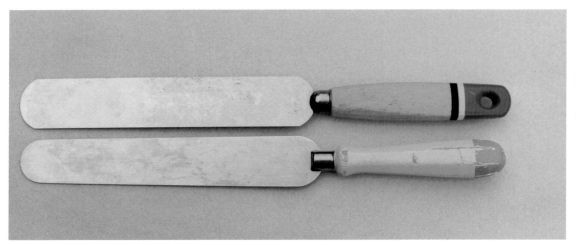

Both spreaders are unmarked, the blue and white handle being more difficult to find but in worn condition. $8-10 each.

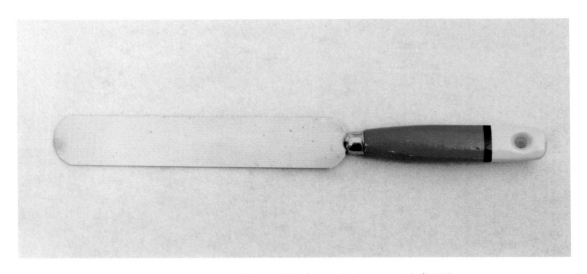

At 11.5" in length the red, white, and black spreader is unmarked. $10-15.

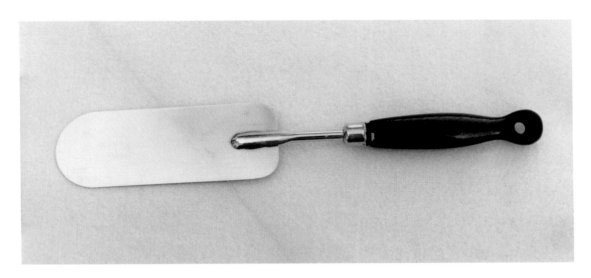

The black spreader has a wider blade and a slightly longer length at 11.75". $7-10.

The bakelite spreader on the bottom is marked stainless steel and still shows pitting. At 12.25" in length it is the longest spreader shown. $15-20 each, $25-30 each if mint.

Strainers

The difference between strainers goes beyond wood, plastic, or bakelite handles. The diameter of the basket can be as small as 2.5" or greater than 8". The mesh can be fine or wide sometimes with an "X" of metal crisscrossing for support. Some baskets have mesh centers with metal around the outside.

Strainers are designed to sit on a bowl, cup, or mug, the handle acting as one contact point. At the other side of the strainer basket there may be two narrow "hooks" or one wide "hook" on which it rests.

Finding a stainer in a handle style being collected should not be difficult as they are plentiful. The reward for hunting is accumulating several sizes that match.

Two matching strainers are 8" long. $10-15 each.

Yellow and green handles are shown in these 10.75" long strainers. $10-15 each.

Three consecutive sizes are grouped together. $5-7 each in worn condition, $10-15 each if mint.

A different yellow and green handle is used on an 8.5" and 11.75" strainer. The worn condition affects value. $5-7 each as shown, $10-15 each if mint.

A single hook is on the end of a 12" long yellow and green handled strainer with much wear. $5-7 as shown, $10-15 if mint.

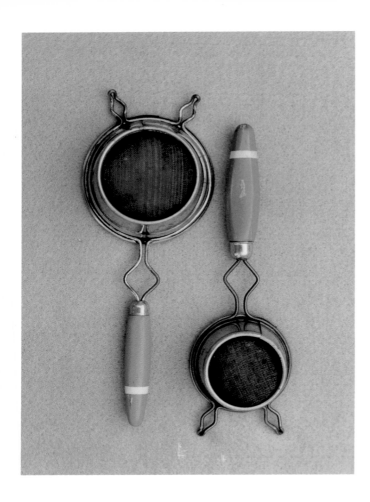

Metal surrounds the mesh centers of matching green handled strainers. The diameter of the top piece is 2.5" and the diameter of the bottom strainer is 3.25". Right $8-10 (some damage to paint), left $10-15.

This strainer has the less common twisted wire connecting to its handle. The ultra-fine mesh and 2.5" diameter make this good for loose tea. $12-15.

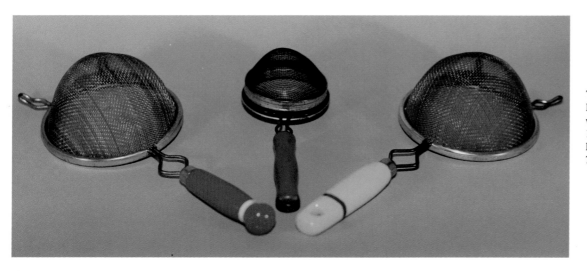

Three strainers exhibit different handle treatments. The yellow with green and red with white are 10.5" long. The solid green handled strainer in the center is 7.5" long. $10-15 each.

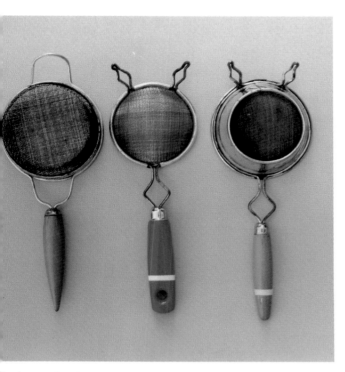

Both green handled strainers are just over 8.5" in length, and the red handled one is 8.25" long. They are all unmarked with fine mesh. $10-15 each.

From left to right the red handled strainers are 8.5, 8.25, and 9" long. Even though they all have a similar paint pattern each handle is unique. $10-12 each.

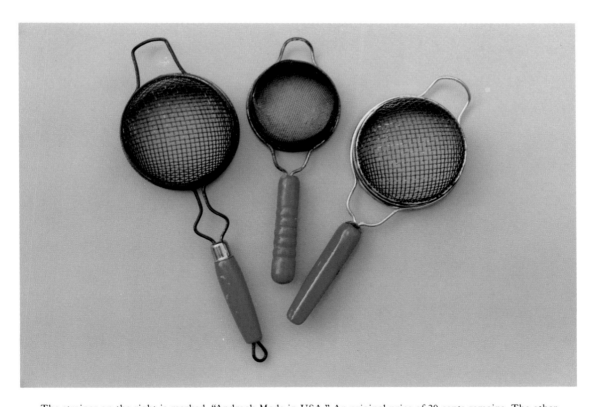

The strainer on the right is marked, "Androck Made in USA." An original price of 20 cents remains. The other strainers are unmarked. All three of these plain red handled strainers have single hooks. $10-12 each.

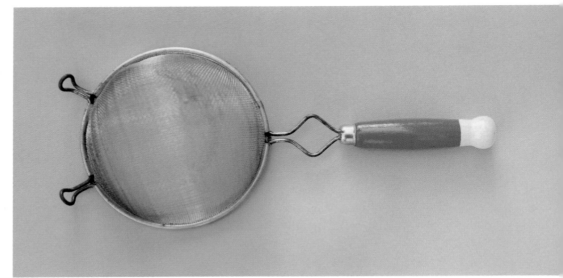

An unmarked red and white strainer is 11.75" long. $10-12.

This unmarked strainer is 12.5" long and 5" across the basket. $10-12.

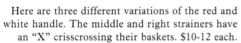

Here are three different variations of the red and white handle. The middle and right strainers have an "X" crisscrossing their baskets. $10-12 each.

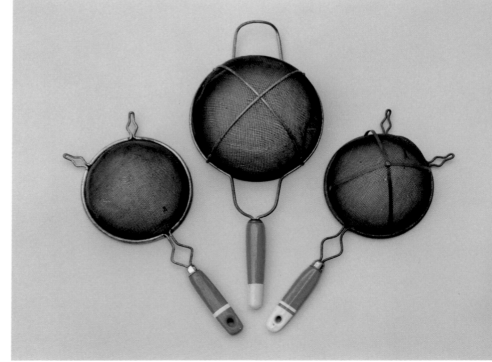

Androck made this strainer which is the largest one pictured. It is 17" long with an 8.25" diameter. $12-15.

The fine-meshed strainer is 8.25" long, and the wide-meshed strainer measures 9" in length. $10-12 each.

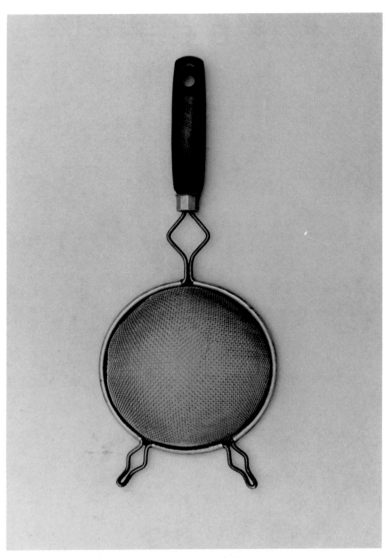

A 4.25" diameter is on an unmarked black handled strainer. It is 10.75" long. $7-10.

Bakelite handled strainers can be found with some searching. Wooden handles are far more common and therefore less expensive. The strainer on the left measures just over 7.5" and the one on the right is 9" long. $30-35 each.

The less popular plain wooden handled strainer on the left is 14.25" long. Androck made the 8" long yellow, turquoise, and black handled strainer in the center. The red and white plastic handled strainer is 13.5" long. Plain handle $3-5, yellow multi-colored handle $15-18, plastic handle $8-10.

Syrups

Syrup dispensers are as useful today as they were in years past. They take a potentially messy task and keep it sanitary and neat with a bit of affordable nostalgia readily found in the marketplace.

With the wide variety of colors, sizes, shapes, handle materials, and mechanisms the choices are almost endless. Space does not permit more than a cross-section of the options available to a collector.

Selection for purchase is usually based on size or color. Many collectors want a particular size to meet their family's consumption needs. Color possibilities, particularly in plastic, are vast so someone wanting a specific hue for a color scheme should eventually meet with success.

When shopping for a syrup dispenser there are two important items to consider. First, make sure the mechanism works easily. Use a thumb to open and close the dispenser noting how easy or difficult the task is. Second, remove the lid and examine the glass for chips or cracks in order to avoid an unpleasant surprise at home.

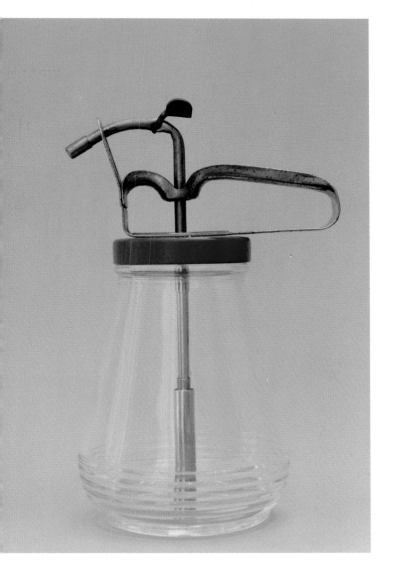

The unmarked syrup dispenser has an intriguing mechanism that operates by pumping. It is almost 7" tall. $25-30.

Federal Tool Corporation from Chicago patented a unique lid for the unmarked base of this syrup dispenser. $15-20.

The grouping presents a variety of bases, lids, and handle treatments. On the left is a pressed glass dispenser with a flip-up lid. The bakelite "bullet" handle in the middle is the most popular syrup dispenser handle. Chrome with simple, unadorned lines graces the syrup on the right. Left $12-15, middle $25-30, right $5-7.

An original "Stop Drip" label remains on a plastic handled syrup dispenser made in Hollywood, California. $15-20 with label, $12-15 without label.

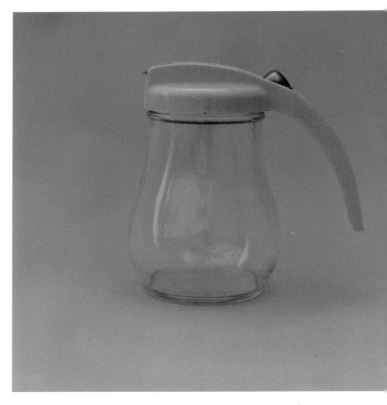

The 4" tall pink topped dispenser is marked "Dripcut 613 106 Made in U.S.A." $8-12.

The syrup on the left has a "Stop Drip" lid in green plastic. On the right is an olive green lid from Federal Tool Corporation in Chicago. Left $12-15, right $8-12.

Three different mechanisms in three different colors are on three different bases of three different sizes. The two lids on the left are marked "Federal Tool Corp." The green lid second from the right is unmarked. This syrup is 4.25" tall. Federal Tool Corporation made the green lid on the far right. The base is marked "Medco NYC 2 USA," and the entire unit is only four inches tall. $8-12 each.

The lid of this syrup is marked "Federal Tool Corp." and the base "Federal Practical Housewares." Both companies are from Chicago. The overall height of this red plastic-lidded dispenser is 5.5". $12-15.

Hazel Atlas made the base of this 9.25" plastic-topped syrup. The lid is unmarked. Tall syrup dispensers command a higher price. $15-20.

A variety of plastic with metal and all plastic lids are on different bases. The 5.75" syrup dispenser on the far left is marked "Federal Tool Corp." Second from the left is a 6" syrup with a Hazel Atlas base. "Federal Tool Corp. Chicago" is embossed on the base of the 6" dispenser that is second from the right. The syrup dispenser on the far right is only 4" tall and marked "Federal Practical Housewares." Far left $25-30, others $8-12 each.

Both yellow-lidded syrups (left and middle) are from Federal Tool Corporation. The off-white dispenser on the right is from Medco Products in New York City. $8-12 each.

Etchings decorate the glass base of an 8.5" bakelite handled syrup. Both the lid and base are unmarked. $25-30.

Dripcut manufactured the 8.5" dispenser with a light green bakelite handle on the left. The 3.25" syrup on the right has a plastic lid. Both the base and lid are marked "Federal Housewares Chicago 45, Illinois." Left $25-30, right $8-12.

The 4.25" syrup dispenser on the left was made by Dripcut. Only patent information marks the lid of the 6" syrup on the right. Its base has a starburst design with "Made in U.S.A. 4" on the bottom. Both dispensers have red bakelite handles. $25-30 each.

All three syrup dispensers have bakelite handles. The red "bullet" handle on the far left was made by Federal Tool Corporation with the most desired handle style of all. It, along with the syrup in the middle, is 5.5" tall. The bulbous syrup dispenser in the middle is unmarked. The green bakelite handle on the right is on a base marked "made in USA." This dispenser is only 4.25" tall. Left (bullet) $25-30, middle $25-30, right $25-30.

Trash Cans

The trash cans presented here are of two styles. The first is an open container often decorated on only one side, and the second is a lidded receptacle with a foot pedal to control this lid.

All of the trash cans here are metal, and most have canister sets and other kitchen pieces that match. Their bright colors perk up a drab task, but a small size of usually under 12" makes them impractical for today's disposable society.

Can you imagine how grandma might react to us treasuring her trash can? It most certainly was the most functional of items receiving minimal care or concern for longevity. Just finding a trash can to match other kitchen metalware is usually enough to excite many collectors. Dents, rust, and other indications of use and/or abuse are often, rightfully overlooked.

Decoware, a name seen on many metal kitchen items, made this 12.25" tall Poppy trash can. $35-40.

Morning Glories decorate this unmarked 9.5" tall trash can. $40-50.

The bright florals of this 11.5" tall unmarked trash can allow it to work with many color schemes. $35-40.

A bouquet of red roses decorate an 11.5" tall unmarked trash can. $25-30.

An unmarked 11.25" tall trash can displays an arrangement of pansies. $35-40.

Decoware manufactured this very popular apple trash can. Made in the U.S.A., it is 12.25" tall. $35-40.

NC Colorware produced a 9.25" trash can with the clover design shown elsewhere in this book. $35-40.

The remains of an original price tag indicate this trash can would have sold for less than one dollar. A gray background color is unusual. It stands 9.25" tall. $25-30.

This unmarked covered trash can stands 13" high. A removable liner with a bail handle acts as the waste receptacle. $75-85 complete with liner.

Whips

Although this section is called "Whips," it includes batter beaters and other multipurposed tools that are able to whip ingredients. As with many of the gadgets previously presented, handles are pictured in wood, plastic, metal, and bakelite.

The design incorporating a coiled wire that zigzags across an oval is the most difficult wire whip to find. This presentation doesn't even include one with a green wooden handle. The "Kitchamajig" marked "Siegler" is still common, so collectors can be particular regarding the handle condition of this item. The three whips pictured last are the most challenging to locate.

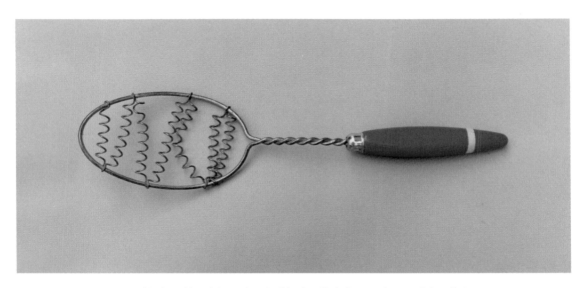

A 12.25" wire whip with a red and white handle is in superior condition. $15-20.

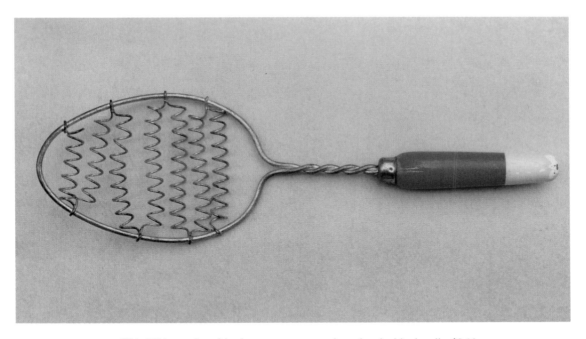

This 11" long wire whip shows some wear on its red and white handle. $8-10.

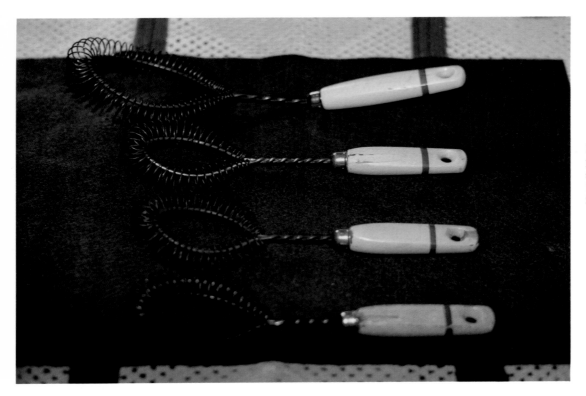

Four wire whips are pictured with yellow handles that have one green stripe. They range in size from 9" to 11.5" with varying degrees of wear. $8-15 each depending on condition.

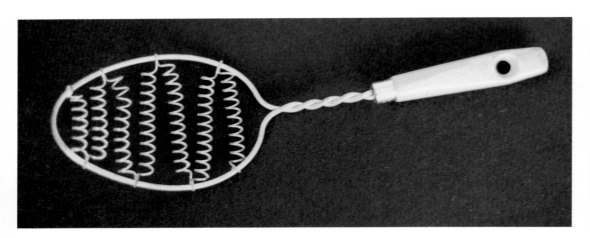

Androck made this yellow handled 11.25" long wire whip. $10-15.

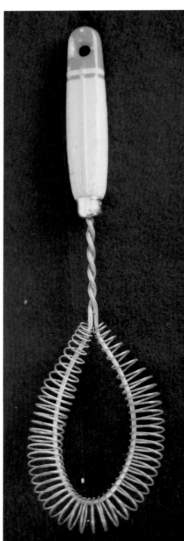

A yellow and green wooden handle is on this 11.75" long wire whip. $8-10 as shown with some wear.

A plastic red and white handle is on this 8.75" long wire whip. $8-12.

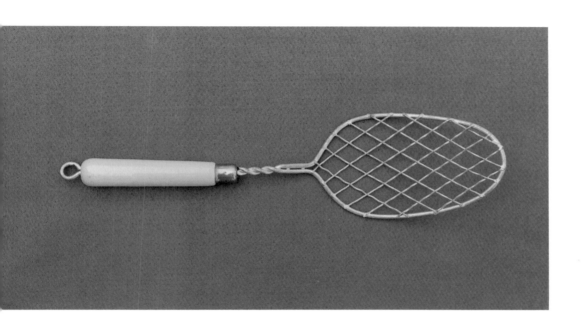

This 11.25" long wire whip exemplifies a different design than the previous pieces. $10-12.

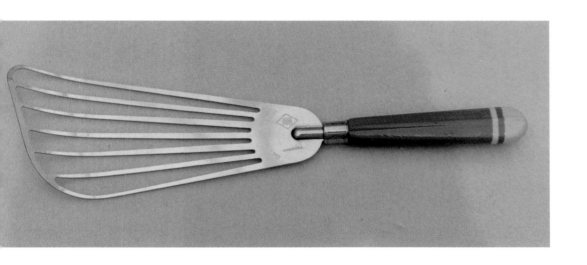

"BATTER BEATER" is inscribed on the chromium plated metal of this A&J product measuring 11" in length. It is in pristine condition. $15-20.

This wip is shown with a yellow handle having one green stripe. There is slight wear on the paint, but the metal is in excellent condition. $8-10.

A&J made this whip with a red bakelite handle. $25-30.

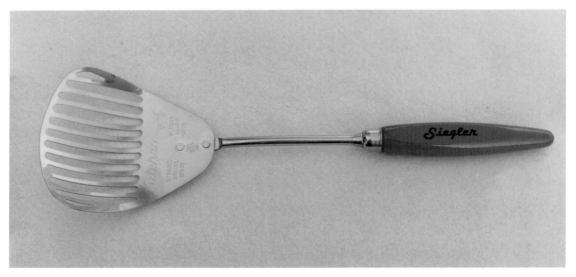

"Siegler" is on a red wooden handled "Kitchamajig." EKCO A&J produced this 12" long gadget that "Strains, Drains, Beats, Blends, Whips, Mixes." $10-15.

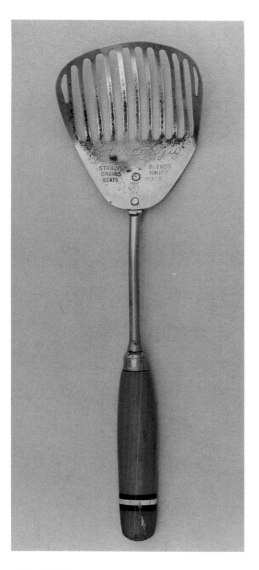

This "Kitchamajig" is identical to the previous one except for handle treatment and condition. $5-7 as shown, $10-12 if mint.

A blue handle is on this 11" long wire spoon that also whips, strains, mixes, and more. $20-25.

This 7.5" long wire whip has a light green wooden knob on the end of its handle. $15-20.

"THE LITTLE KITCHEN GEM 10 IN 1 COMBINATION KITCHEN TOOL" was free with a jar or can of "HIP-O-LITE." The ten tasks it was designed to do include whipping cream. This versatile 8" long gadget is from the Hipolite Company of St. Louis, Missouri. $15-20 with package, $8-10 without package.

Bibliography

Florence, Gene. *Kitchen Glassware of the Depression Years.* Paducah, Kentucky: Collector Books, 1995.

Huxford, Sharon and Bob., ed. *Schroeder's Antiques Price Guide.* Paducah, Kentucky: Collector Books, 1995.

Kilgo, Garry and Dale and Wilkins, Jerry and Gail. *A Collector's Guide to Anchor Hocking's Fire-King Glassware.* Addison, Alabama: K&W Collectibles Publisher, 1991.

Kovel, Ralph and Terry. *Kovels' Antiques & Collectibles Price List 1996.* New York: Crown Trade Paperbacks, 1996.

Lifshey, Earl. *The Housewares Story.* Chicago: National Housewares Manufacturers Association, 1973.

Rogove, Susan Tobier and Steinhauer, Marcia Buan. *Pyrex by Corning: A Collector's Guide.* Marietta, Ohio: Antique Publication, 1993.